9-16-74

POSTHUMOUS WORKS

OF

MARY WOLLSTONECRAFT GODWIN

VOLUME II

Also by MARY WOLLSTONECRAFT GODWIN

Thoughts on the Education of Daughters [1787]

[*MARY WOLLSTONECRAFT GODWIN*]

POSTHUMOUS WORKS

OF THE

AUTHOR

OF

A VINDICATION OF THE RIGHTS OF WOMAN

[1798]

Four Volumes in Two

VOLUME II

AUGUSTUS M. KELLEY • PUBLISHERS
CLIFTON 1972

First Edition 1798

(*London* : *Printed for* J. Johnson, *No. 72, St. Paul's Church-Yard* ; and **G. G.** & J. Robinson, *Paternoster-Row*, 1798)

Reprinted 1972 by

AUGUSTUS M. KELLEY PUBLISHERS

Reprints of Economic Classics

Clifton New Jersey 07012

I S B N 0 678 00900 7

L C N 70-187780

PRINTED IN THE UNITED STATES OF AMERICA

by SENTRY PRESS, NEW YORK, N. Y. 10013

POSTHUMOUS WORKS

OF

MARY WOLLSTONECRAFT GODWIN.

VOL. III.

POSTHUMOUS WORKS

OF THE

AUTHOR

OF A

VINDICATION OF THE RIGHTS OF WOMAN.

IN FOUR VOLUMES.

VOL. III.

LONDON:

PRINTED FOR J. JOHNSON, NO. 72, ST. PAUL'S
CHURCH-YARD; AND G. G. AND J. ROBINSON,
PATERNOSTER-ROW.
1798.

LETTERS

AND

MISCELLANEOUS PIECES.

IN TWO VOLUMES.

VOL. I.

PREFACE.

THE following Letters may poſſibly be found to contain the fineſt examples of the language of ſentiment and paſſion ever preſented to the world. They bear a ſtriking reſemblance to the celebrated romance of Werter, though the incidents to which they relate are of a very different caſt. Probably the readers to whom Werter is incapable of affording pleaſure, will receive no delight from the preſent publication. The editor apprehends

that,

that, in the judgment of thofe beft qualified to decide upon the comparifon, thefe Letters will be admitted to have the fuperiority over the fiction of Goethe. They are the offspring of a glowing imagination, and a heart penetrated with the paffion it effays to defcribe.

To the feries of letters conftituting the principal article in thefe two volumes, are added various pieces, none of which, it is hoped, will be found difcreditable to the talents of the author. The flight fragment of Letters on the Management of Infants, may be thought a trifle ; but it feems to have fome value, as prefenting to us with vividnefs the intention of the writer on

this

this important fubject. The publication of a few felect Letters to **Mr. Johnfon**, appeared to be at once a juft monument to the fincerity of his friendfhip, and a valuable and interefting fpecimen of the mind of the writer. The Letter on the Prefent Character of the French Nation, the Extract of the Cave of Fancy, a Tale, and the Hints for the Second Part of the Rights of Woman, may, I believe, fafely be left to fpeak for themfelves. The Effay on Poetry and our Relifh for the Beauties of Nature, appeared in the Monthly Magazine for April laft, and is the only piece in this collection which has previoufly found its way to the prefs.

CONTENTS.

ERRATA.

Page 10. line 8, *for* I write you, *read* I write to you.
—— 20. — 9, *read* bring them to ——.
—— 146, — 2 from the bottom, after over, infert
a comma.

LETTERS.

LETTER I.

MY dear love, after making my
arrangements for our fnug dinner to-
day, I have been taken by ftorm,
and obliged to promife to dine, at
an early hour, with the Mifs ——s,
the *only* day they intend to pafs here.
I fhall however leave the key in the
door, and hope to find you at my
fire-fide when I return, about eight
o'clock. Will you not wait for poor
Joan?—whom you will find better, and

till

till then think very affectionately of
her.

Yours, truly,

* * * *

I am fitting down to dinner; fo do
not fend an anfwer.

LETTER II.

Paft Twelve o'Clock, Monday night.
[Auguft.]

I OBEY an emotion of my heart,
which made me think of wifhing thee,
my love, good-night! before I go to
reft, with more tendernefs than I can
to-morrow, when writing a hafty line
or two under Colonel ———'s eye. You
can fcarcely imagine with what pleafure I anticipate the day, when we are

to

to begin almoſt to live together; and you would ſmile to hear how many plans of employment I have in my head, now that I am confident my heart has found peace in your boſom.—Cheriſh me with that dignified tendernefs, which I have only found in you; and your own dear girl will try to keep under a quicknefs of feeling, that has ſometimes given you pain—Yes, I will be *good*, that I may deſerve to be happy; and whilſt you love me, I cannot again fall into the miſerable ſtate, which rendered life a burthen almoſt too heavy to be borne.

But, good-night!—God blefs you! Sterne ſays, that is equal to a kifs—yet I would rather give you the kifs into the bargain, glowing with gratitude to Heaven, and affection to you. I like the word affection, becauſe it ſignifies

ſomething

ſomething habitual; and we are ſoon to meet, to try whether we have mind enough to keep our hearts warm.

                       * * * *

I will be at the barrier a little after ten o'clock to-morrow*.—Yours—

L E T T E R III.

Wedneſday Morning.

You have often called me, dear girl, but you would now ſay good, did you know how very attentive I have been to the —— ever ſince I came to Paris. I am not however going to trouble

---

    * The child is in a ſubſequent letter called the " barrier girl," probably from a ſuppoſition that ſhe owed her exiſtence to this interview.

                          EDITOR.

                             you

you with the account, becaufe I like to fee your eyes praife me; and, Milton infinuates, that, during fuch recitals, there are interruptions, not ungrateful to the heart, when the honey that drops from the lips is not merely words.

Yet, I fhall not (let me tell you before thefe people enter, to force me to huddle away my letter) be content with only a kifs of DUTY—you *muſt* be glad to fee me—becaufe you are glad—or I will make love to the *ſhade* of Mirabeau, to whom my heart continually turned, whilft I was talking with Madame ——, forcibly telling me, that it will ever have fufficient warmth to love, whether I will or not, fentiment, though I fo highly refpect principle.——

Not that I think Mirabeau utterly devoid of principles—Far from it—and, if I had not begun to form a new theory

ory

ory refpecting men, I fhould, in the vanity of my heart, have *imagined* that *I*
could have made fomething of his——
it was compofed of fuch materials——
Hufh! here they come—and love flies
away in the twinkling of an eye, leaving a little brufh of his wing on my
pale cheeks.

I hope to fee Dr. —— this morning;
I am going to Mr.——'s to meet him.
——, and fome others, are invited to
dine with us to-day; and to-morrow I
am to fpend the day with ——.

I fhall probably not be able to return
to —— to-morrow; but it is no matter, becaufe I muft take a carriage, I
have fo many books, that I immediately want, to take with me.—On Friday then I fhall expect you to dine
with me—and, if you come a little before dinner, it is fo long fince I have

feen

feen you, you will not be fcolded by yours affectionately

* * * *

LETTER IV*.

Friday Morning [September.]

A MAN, whom a letter from Mr.——previoufly announced, called here yefterday for the payment of a draft; and, as he feemed difappointed at not finding you at home, I fent him to Mr.——. I have fince feen him, and he tells me that he has fettled the bufinefs.

So much for bufinefs!—May I venture to talk a little longer about lefs weighty affairs?—How are you?—I

---

* This and the thirteen following letters appear to have been written during a feparation of feveral months; the date, Paris.

have

have been following you all along the
road this comfortlefs weather; for,
when I am abfent from thofe I love, my
imagination is as lively, as if my fenfes
had never been gratified by their prefence—I was going to fay careffes—and
why fhould I not? I have found out
that I have more mind than you, in one
refpect; becaufe I can, without any
violent effort of reafon, find food for
love in the fame object, much longer
than you can.—The way to my fenfes
is through my heart; but, forgive me!
I think there is fometimes a fhorter cut
to yours.

With ninety-nine men out of a hundred, a very fufficient dafh of folly is
neceffary to render a woman *piquante*, a
foft word for defirable; and, beyond
thefe cafual ebullitions of fympathy,
few look for enjoyment by foftering a

paffion

paſſion in their hearts. One reaſon, in ſhort, why I wiſh my whole ſex to be-come wiſer, is, that the fooliſh ones may not, by their preſty folly, rob thoſe whoſe ſenſibility keeps down their va-nity, of the few roſes that afford them ſome ſolace in the thorny road of life.

I do not know how I fell into theſe reflections, excepting one thought pro-duced it—that theſe continual ſepara-tions were neceſſary to warm your af-fection.—Of late, we are always ſepa-rating.—Crack!—crack!—and away you go.—This joke wears the ſallow caſt of thought; for, though I began to write cheerfully, ſome melancholy tears have found their way into my eyes, that linger there, whilſt a glow of tenderneſs at my heart whiſpers that you are one of the beſt creatures in the world.— Pardon then the vagaries of a mind,

that

that has been almoſt " crazed by care," as well as " croſſed in hapleſs love," and bear with me a *little* longer !—When we are ſettled in the country together, more duties will open before me, and my heart, which now, trembling into peace, is agitated by every emotion that awakens the remembrance of old griefs, will learn to reſt on yours, with that dignity your character, not to talk of my own, demands.

Take care of yourſelf—and write ſoon to your own girl (you may add dear, if you pleaſe) who ſincerely loves you, and will try to convince you of it, by becoming happier.

                          * * * *

LETTER

LETTER V.

Sunday Night.

I HAVE juft received your letter, and feel as if I could not go to bed tranquilly without faying a few words in reply— merely to tell you, that my mind is ferene, and my heart affectionate.

Ever fince you laft faw me inclined to faint, I have felt fome gentle twitches, which make me begin to think, that I am nourifhing a creature who will foon be fenfible of my care.—This thought has not only produced an overflowing of tendernefs to you, but made me very attentive to calm my mind and take exercife, left I fhould deftroy an object, in whom we are to have a mutual intereft, you know. Yefterday—do not fmile!—finding that I had hurt myfelf

by

by lifting precipitately a large log of
wood, I fat down in an agony, till I felt
thofe faid twitches again.

Are you very bufy?

———   ———   ———   ———   ———   ———   ———

———   ———   ———   ———   ———   ———   ———

———   ———   ———   ———   ———   ———   ———

———   ———   ———   ———   ———   ———   ———

———   ———   ———   ———   ———   ———   ———

So you may reckon on its being finifhed
foon, though not before you come
home, unlefs you are detained longer
than I now allow myfelf to believe you
will.—

Be that as it may, write to me, my
beft love, and bid me be patient—
kindly—and the expreffions of kindnefs
will again beguile the time, as fweetly
as they have done to-night.—Tell me
alfo over and over again, that your
happinefs (and you deferve to be
happy!)

happy!) is clofely connected with mine, and I will try to diffipate, as they rife, the fumes of former difcontent, that have too often clouded the funfhine, which you have endeavoured to diffufe through my mind. God blefs you! Take care of yourfelf, and remember with tendernefs your affectionate

* * * *

I am going to reft very happy, and you have made me fo.—This is the kindeft good-night I can utter.

LETTER

LETTER VI.

Friday Morning.

I am glad to find that other people can be unreafonable, as well as myfelf — for be it known to thee, that I anfwered thy *firſt* letter, the very night it reached me (Sunday), though thou couldſt not receive it before Wednefday, becaufe it was not fent off till the next day.—There is a full, true, and particular account.—

Yet I am not angry with thee, my love, for I think that it is a proof of ſtupidity, and likewife of a milk-and-water affection, which comes to the fame thing, when the temper is governed by a fquare and compafs.—There is nothing picturefque in this ſtraight-lined

lined equality, and the paffions always give grace to the actions.

Recollection now makes my heart bound to thee; but, it is not to thy money-getting face, though I cannot be feriously difpleafed with the exertion which increafes my efteem, or rather is what I fhould have expected from thy character.—No; I have thy honeft countenance before me—Pop—relaxed by tendernefs; a little—little wounded by my whims; and thy eyes gliftening with fympathy.—Thy lips then feel fofter than foft—and I reft my cheek on thine, forgetting all the world.—I have not left the hue of love out of the picture—the rofy glow; and fancy has fpread it over my own cheeks, I believe, for I feel them burning, whilft a delicious tear trembles in my eye, that would be all your own, if a grateful

grateful emotion directed to the Father of nature, who has made me thus alive to happinefs, did not give more warmth to the fentiment it divides—I muft paufe a moment.

Need I tell you that I am tranquil after writing thus?—I do not know why, but I have more confidence in your affection, when abfent, than prefent; nay, I think that you muft love me, for, in the fincerity of my heart let me fay it, I believe I deferve your tendernefs, becaufe I am true, and have a degree of fenfibility that you can fee and relifh.

Yours fincerely

* * * *

LETTER

LETTER VII.

Sunday Morning [December 29.]

You feem to have taken up your abode at H——. Pray fir! when do you think of coming home? or, to write very confiderately, when will bufinefs permit you? I fhall expect (as the country people fay in England) that you will make a *power* of money to indemnify me for your abfence.

— — — — — — —
— — — — — — —
— — — — — — —
— — — — — — —
— — — — — — —
— — — — — — —
— — — — — — —

Well!

Well! but, my love, to the old ſtory—
am I to ſee you this week, or this
month?—I do not know what you are
about—for, as you did not tell me, I
would not aſk Mr. ——, who is generally pretty communicative.

I long to ſee Mrs. ——; not to
hear from you, ſo do not give yourſelf
airs, but to get a letter from Mr. ——.
And I am half angry with you for not
informing me whether ſhe had brought
one with her or not.—On this ſcore I
will cork up ſome of the kind things
that were ready to drop from my pen,
which has never been dipt in gall when
addreſſing you; or, will only ſuffer an
exclamation—" The creature!" or a
kind look, to eſcape me, when I paſs
the ſlippers—which I could not remove
from my *ſalle* door, though they are
not the handſomeſt of their kind.

Be

Be not too anxious to get money!—
for nothing worth having is to be pur-
chafed. God blefs you.

Yours affectionately

* * * *

LETTER VIII.

Monday Night [December 30.]

My beft love, your letter to-night
was particularly grateful to my heart,
depreffed by the letters I received by
———, for he brought me feveral, and
the parcel of books directed to Mr.
——— was for me. Mr. ———'s
letter was long and very affectionate;
but the account he gives me of his own
affairs,

affairs, though he obvioufly makes the
beft of them, has vexed me.

A melancholy letter from my fifter
———— has alfo harraffed my mind—
that from my brother would have given
me fincere pleafure; but for — —

— — — — — —
— — — — — —
— — — — — —
— — — — — —
— — — — — —
— — — — — —
— — — — — —
— — — — — —
— — — — — —

There is a fpirit of independence in
his letter, that will pleafe you; and you
fhall fee it, when we are once more over
the fire together.—I think that you
would hail him as a brother, with one
                                        of

of your tender looks, when your heart
not only gives a luftre to your eye, but
a dance of playfulnefs, that he would
meet with a glow half made up of bafh-
fulnefs, and a defire to pleafe the——
where fhall I find a word to exprefs
the relationfhip which fubfifts between
us?—Shall I afk the little twitcher?——
But I have dropt half the fentence
that was to tell you how much he
would be inclined to love the man loved
by his fifter. I have been fancying myfelf fitting between you, ever fince I
began to write, and my heart has leaped
at the thought!—You fee how I chat
to you.

I. did not receive your letter till I
came home; and I did not expect it,
for the poft came in much later than
ufual. It was a cordial to me—and I
wanted one.

Mr.

Mr. —— tells me that he has written
again and again.—Love him a little !—
It would be a kind of feparation, if you
did not love thofe I love.

There was fo much confiderate tendernefs in your epiftle to-night, that, if
it has not made you dearer to me, it has
made me forcibly feel how very dear
you are to me, by charming away half
my cares.

Yours affectionately

* * * *

LETTER IX.

Tuefday Morning [December 31.]

Though I have juft fent a letter off,
yet, as captain —— offers to take one,
I am not willing to let him go without
a kind greeting, becaufe trifles of this
fort,

fort, without having any effect on my mind, damp my fpirits :—and you, with all your ftruggles to be manly, have fome of this fame fenfibility.—Do not bid it begone, for I love to fee it ftriving to mafter your features; befides, thefe kind of fympathies are the life of affection: and why, in cultivating our underftandings, fhould we try to dry up thefe fprings of pleafure, which gufh out to give a frefhnefs to days browned by care!

The books fent to me are fuch as we may read together; fo I fhall not look into them till you return; when you fhall read, whilft I mend my ftock-ings.

Yours truly

* * * *

LETTER

LETTER X.

Wednesday Night [January 1.]

As I have been, you tell me, three days without writing, I ought not to complain of two : yet, as I expected to receive a letter this afternoon, I am hurt ; and why should I, by concealing it, affect the heroifm I do not feel?

I hate commerce. How differently muft ———'s head and heart be organized from mine! You will tell me, that exertions are neceffary : I am weary of them! The face of things, public and private, vexes me. The " peace" and clemency which feemed to be dawning a few days ago, difappear again. " I am fallen," as Milton faid, " on evil days;" for I really believe

that

that Europe will be in a ftate of con-
vulfion, during half a century at leaft.
Life is but a labour of patience: it is
always rolling a great ftone up a hill;
for, before a perfon can find a refting-
place, imagining it is lodged, down it
comes again, and all the work is to be
done over anew!

Should I attempt to write any more,
I could not change the ftrain. My head
aches, and my heart is heavy. The
world appears an "unweeded garden,"
where "things rank and vile" flourifh
beft.

If you do not return foon—or, which
is no fuch mighty matter, talk of it—
I will throw your flippers out at
window, and be off—nobody knows
where.

＊ ＊ ＊ ＊

Finding

Finding that I was obferved, I told the good women, the two Mrs. ———s, fimply that I was with child: and let them ftare! and ———, and ———, nay, all the world, may know it for aught I care!—Yet I wifh to avoid ———'s coarfe jokes.

Confidering the care and anxiety a woman muft have about a child before it comes into the world, it feems to me, by a *natural right*, to belong to her. When men get immerfed in the world, they feem to lofe all fenfations, excepting thofe neceffary to continue or produce life!—Are thefe the privileges of reafon? Amongft the feathered race, whilft the hen keeps the young warm, her mate ftays by to cheer her; but it is fufficient for man to condefcend to get a child, in order to claim it.—A man is a tyrant!

You

You may now tell me, that, if it were not for me, you would be laughing away with fome honeft fellows in L—n. The cafual exercife of focial fympathy would not be fufficient for me—I fhould not think fuch an heartlefs life worth preferving.—It is neceffary to be in good-humour with you, to be pleafed with the world.

———————

Thurfday Morning.

I was very low-fpirited laft night, ready to quarrel with your cheerful temper, which makes abfence eafy to you.—And, why fhould I mince the the matter? I was offended at your not even mentioning it.—I do not want to be loved like a goddefs; but I wifh to be neceffary to you. God blefs you*!

* Some further letters, written during the remainder of the week, in a fimilar ftrain to the preceding, appear to have been deftroyed by the perfon to whom they were addreffed.

LETTER

LETTER XI.

Monday Night.

I HAVE juft received your kind and rational letter, and would fain hide my face, glowing with fhame for my folly. —I would hide it in your bofom, if you would again open it to me, and neftle clofely till you bade my fluttering heart be ftill, by faying that you forgave me. With eyes overflowing with tears, and in the humbleft attitude, I intreat you.—Do not turn from me, for indeed I love you fondly, and have been very wretched, fince the night I was fo cruelly hurt by thinking that you had no confidence in me——

It is time for me to grow more reafonable, a few more of thefe caprices of fenfibility would deftroy me. I have,

in

in fact, been very much indifpofed for
a few days paft, and the notion that I
was tormenting, or perhaps killing, a
poor little animal, about whom I am
grown anxious and tender, now I feel
it alive, made me worfe. My bowels
have been dreadfully difordered, and
every thing I ate or drank difagreed
with my ftomach; ftill I feel intimations
of its exiftence, though they have been
fainter.

Do you think that the creature goes
regularly to fleep? I am ready to afk as
many queftions as Voltaire's Man of
Forty Crowns. Ah! do not continue to
be angry with me! You perceive that I
am already fmiling through my tears—
You have lightened my heart, and my
frozen fpirits are melting into playfulnefs.

Write the moment you receive this.
I fhall

I ſhall count the minutes. But drop
not an angry word—I cannot now bear
it. Yet, if you think I deſerve a ſcold-
ing (it does not admit of a queſtion, I
grant), wait till you come back—and
then, if you are angry one day, I ſhall
be ſure of ſeeing you the next.

——— did not write to you, I ſuppoſe, becauſe he talked of going to
H———. Hearing that I was ill, he called
very kindly on me, not dreaming that
it was ſome words that he incautiouſly
let fall, which rendered me ſo.

God bleſs you, my love; do not ſhut
your heart againſt a return of tenderneſs; and, as I now in fancy cling to
you, be more than ever my ſupport.—
Feel but as affectionate when you read
this letter, as I did writing it, and you
will make happy, your

* * * *

LETTER

LETTER XII.

Wednefday Morning.

I WILL never, if I am not entirely cured of quarrelling, begin to encourage " quick-coming fancies," when we are feparated. Yefterday, my love, I could not open your letter for fome time; and, though it was not half as fevere as I merited, it threw me into fuch a fit of trembling, as ferioufly alarmed me. I did not, as you may fuppofe, care for a little pain on my own account; but all the fears which I have had for a few days paft, returned with frefh force. This morning I am better; will you not be glad to hear it? You perceive that forrow has almoft made a child of me, and that I want to be foothed to peace.

One thing you miftake in my cha- racter,

racter, and imagine that to be coldnefs which is juft the contrary. For, when I am hurt by the perfon moft dear to me, I muft let out a whole torrent of emotions, in which tendernefs would be uppermoft, or ftifle them altogether; and it appears to me almoft a duty to ftifle them, when I imagine *that I am treated with coldnefs.*

I am afraid that I have vexed you, my own ———. I know the quicknefs of your feelings—and let me, in the fincerity of my heart, affure you, there is nothing I would not fuffer to make you happy. My own happinefs wholly depends on you—and, knowing you, when my reafon is not clouded, I look forward to a rational profpect of as much felicity as the earth affords—with a little dafh of rapture into the bargain, if you will look at me, when we meet

again,

again, as you have fometimes greeted,
your humbled, yet moft affectionate

* * * *

LETTER XIII.

Thurfday Night.

I HAVE been wifhing the time away,
my kind love, unable to reft till I knew
that my penitential letter had reached
your hand—and this afternoon, when
your tender epiftle of Tuefday gave
fuch exquifite pleafure to your poor
fick girl, her heart fmote her to think
that you were ftill to receive another
cold one.—Burn it alfo, my ——; yet
do not forget that even thofe letters
were full of love; and I fhall ever recollect, that you did not wait to be
mollified by my penitence, before you
took me again to your heart.

I have

I have been unwell, and would not, now I am recovering, take a journey, becaufe I have been ferioufly alarmed and angry with myfelf, dreading continually the fatal confequence of my folly.--But, fhould you think it right to remain at H—, I fhall find fome opportunity, in the courfe of a fortnight, or lefs perhaps, to come to you, and before then I fhall be ftrong again.—Yet do not be uneafy! I am really better, and never took fuch care of myfelf, as I have done fince you reftored my peace of mind. The girl is come to warm my bed—fo I will tenderly fay, good night! and write a line or two in the morning.

Morning.

I wish you were here to walk with me this fine morning! yet your abfence fhall not prevent me. I have ftayed at home too much; though, when

when I was fo dreadfully out of fpirits, I was carelefs of every thing.

I will now fally forth (you will go with me in my heart) and try whether this fine bracing a r will not give the vigour to the poor babe, it had, before I fo inconfiderately gave way to the grief that deranged my bowels, and gave a turn to my whole fyftem.

Yours truly

* * * * * * * * *

LETTER

LETTER XIV.

Saturday Morning.

THE two or three letters, which I have written to you lately, my love, will ferve as an anfwer to your explanatory one. I cannot but refpect your motives and conduct. I always refpected them; and was only hurt, by what feemed to me a want of confidence, and confequently affection.—I thought alfo, that if you were obliged to ftay three months at H—, I might as well have been with you.—Well! well, what fignifies what I brooded over—Let us now be friends!

I fhall probably receive a letter from you to-day, fealing my pardon—and I will be careful not to torment you with

my

my querulous humours, at leaft, till I
fee you again. Act as circumftances
direct, and I will not enquire when
they will permit you to return, convinced that you will haften to your
* * * *, when you have attained (or
loft fight of) the object of your journey.

What a picture have you fketched of
our fire-fide! Yes, my love, my fancy
was inftantly at work, and I found my
head on your fhoulder, whilft my eyes
were fixed on the little creatures that
were clinging about your knees. I did
not abfolutely determine that there
fhould be fix—if you have not fet your
heart on this round number.

I am going to dine with Mrs, ——.
I have not been to vifit her fince the
firft day fhe came to Paris. I wifh
indeed to be out in the air as much as
I can; for the exercife I have taken
thefe

thefe two or three days paft, has been
of fuch fervice to me, that I hope
fhortly to tell you, that I am quite well.
I have fcarcely flept before laft night,
and then not much.—The two Mrs.
————s have been very anxious and
tender.

Yours truly

* * * *

I need not defire you to give the
colonel a good bottle of wine.

LETTER XV.

Sunday Morning.

I wrote to you yefterday, my ——;
but, finding that the colonel is ftill de
tained (for his paffport was forgotten at
the office yefterday) I am not willing to

let

let fo many days elapfe without your hearing from me, after having talked of illnefs and apprehenfions.

I cannot boaft of being quite recovered, yet I am (I muft ufe my York-fhire phrafe; for, when my heart is warm, pop come the expreffions of, childhood into my head) fo *lightfome*, that I think it will not *go badly with me.*—And nothing fhall be wanting on my part, I affure you; for I am urged on, not only by an enlivened affection for you, but by a new-born tendernefs that plays cheerly round my dilating heart.

I was therefore, in defiance of cold, and dirt, out in the air the greater part of yefterday; and, if I get over this evening without a return of the fever that has tormented me, I fhall talk no more of illnefs. I have promifed the

little

little creature, that its mother, who
ought to cherifh it, will not again
plague it, and begged it to pardon me;
and, fince I could not hug either it or
you to my breaft, I have to my heart.—
I am afraid to read over this prattle—
but it is only for your eye.

I have been ferioufly vexed, to find
that, whilft you were harraffed by im-
pediments in your undertakings, I was
giving you additional uneafinefs.—If
you can make any of your plans anfwer
—it is well, I do not think a *little* money
inconvenient; but, fhould they fail, we
will ftruggle cheerfully together—
drawn clofer by the pinching blafts of
poverty.

Adieu, my love! Write often to
your poor girl, and write long letters;
for I not only like them for being longer,
but becaufe more heart fteals into them;
and

and I am happy to catch your heart whenever I can.

Yours sincerely

* * * *

LETTER XVI.

Tuesday Morning.

I SEIZE this opportunity to inform you, that I am to set out on Thursday with Mr. ————, and hope to tell you soon (on your lips) how glad I shall be to see you. I have just got my passport, so I do not foresee any impediment to my reaching H——, to bid you good-night next Friday in my new apartment —where I am to meet you and love, in spite of care, to smile me to sleep— for I have not caught much rest since we parted.

You

You have, by your tendernefs and worth, twifted yourfelf more artfully round my heart, than I fuppofed pof-fible.—Let me indulge the thought, that I have thrown out fome tendrils to cling to the elm by which I wifh to be fupported.—This is talking a new lan-guage for me!—But, knowing that I am not a parafite-plant, I am willing to receive the proofs of affection, that every pulfe replies to, when I think of being once more in the fame houfe with you.—God blefs you!

Yours truly

* * * *

LETTER

LETTER XVII.

Wednefday Morning.

I ONLY fend this as an *avant-coureur*, without jack-boots, to tell you, that I am again on the wing, and hope to be with you a few hours after you receive it. I fhall find you well, and compofed, I am fure ; or, more properly fpeaking, cheerful.—What is the reafon that my fpirits are not as manageable as yours? Yet, now I think of it, I will not allow that your temper is even, though I have promifed myfelf, in order to obtain my own forgivenefs, that I will not ruffle it for a long, long time—I am afraid to fay never.

Farewell for a moment !—Do not forget

forget that I am driving towards you in perfon! My mind, unfettered, has flown to you long fince, or rather has never left you.

I am well, and have no apprehenfion that I fhall find the journey too fatiguing, when I follow the lead of my heart.—With my face turned to H— my fpirits will not fink—and my mind has always hitherto enabled my body to do whatever I wifhed.

Yours affectionately

* * * *

LETTER

LETTER XVIII.

H—, Thurſday Morning, March 12.

WE are ſuch creatures of habit, my love, that, though I cannot ſay I was ſorry, childiſhly ſo, for your going, when I knew that you were to ſtay ſuch a ſhort time, and I had a plan of employment; yet I could not ſleep.—I turned to your ſide of the bed, and tried to make the moſt of the comfort of the pillow, which you uſed to tell me I was churliſh about; but all would not do.—I took neverthelefs my walk before breakfaſt, though the weather was not very inviting—and here I am, wiſhing you a finer day, and ſeeing you peep over my ſhoulder, as I write, with one of your kindeſt looks—when your

eyes

eyes gliften, and a fuffufion creeps over your relaxing features.

But I do not mean to dally with you this morning---So God blefs you! Take care of yourfelf—and fometimes fold to your heart your affectionate

* ● * *

LETTER XIX.

DO not call me ftupid, for leaving on the table the little bit of paper I was to inclofe.—-This comes of being in love at the fag-end of a letter of bufi-nefs.—You know, you fay, they will not chime together.—I had got you by the fire-fide, with the *gigot* fmoking on the board, to lard your poor bare ribs —and behold, I clofed my letter with-

out

out taking the paper up, that was directly under my eyes!—What had I got in them to render me fo blind?—I give you leave to anfwer the queftion, if you will not fcold; for I am

Yours moft affectionately

* * * *

LETTER XX.

Sunday, Auguft 17.

— — — — — — —

— — — — — — —

— — — — — — —

I have promifed ———— to go with him to his country-houfe, where he is now permitted to dine—I, and the little darling, to be fure *—whom I cannot

* The child fpoken of in fome preceding letters, had now been born a confiderable time.

help

help kiffing with more fondnefs, fince
you left us. I think I fhall enjoy the
fine profpect, and that it will rather
enliven, than fatiate my imagination.

I have called on Mrs. ————. She
has the manners of a gentlewoman,
with a dafh of the eafy French coquetry,
which renders her *piquante*.—But *Mon-
fieur* her hufband, whom nature never
dreamed of cafting in either the mould
of a gentleman or lover, makes but an
aukward figure in the foreground of
the picture.

The H——s are very ugly, without
doubt—and the houfe fmelt of commerce from top to toe—fo that his
abortive attempt to difplay tafte, only
proved it to be one of the things not to
be bought with gold. I was in a room
a moment alone, and my attention was
attracted by the *pendule*——A nymph was
offering

offering up her vows before a fmoking
altar, to a fat-bottomed Cupid (faving
your prefence), who was kicking his
heels in the air.—Ah! kick on, thought
I; for the demon of traffic will ever
fright away the loves and graces, that
ftreak with the rofy beams of infant
fancy the *fombre* day of life—whilft the
imagination, not allowing us to fee
things as they are, enables us to catch
a hafty draught of the running ftream
of delight, the thirft for which feems to
be given only to tantalize us.

But I am philofophizing; nay, perhaps you will call me fevere, and bid
me let the fquare-headed money-getters
alone.—Peace to them! though none
of the focial fprites (and there are not a
few of different defcriptions, who fport
about the various inlets to my heart)
gave me a twitch to reftrain my pen.

I have

I have been writing on, expecting poor —————— to come; for, when I began, I merely thought of bufinefs; and, as this is the idea that moft naturally affociates with your image, I wonder I ftumbled on any other.

Yet, as common life, in my opinion, is fcarcely worth having, even with a *gigot* every day, and a pudding added thereunto, I will allow you to cultivate my judgment, if you will permit me to keep alive the fentiments in your heart, which may be termed romantic, becaufe, the offspring of the fenfes and the imagination, they refemble the mother more than the father *, when they produce the fuffufion I admire.— In fpite of icy age, I hope ftill to fee it,

---

* She means, " the latter more than the former."
                                    EDITOR.

if

if you have not determined only to eat and drink, and be ftupidly ufeful to the ftupid—

     Yours

       * * * ●

LETTER XXI.

H—, Auguft 19, Tuefday.

I RECEIVED both your letters to-day —I had reckoned on hearing from you yeftcrday, therefore was difappointed, though I imputed your filence to the right caufe. I intended anfwering your kind letter immediately, that you might have felt the pleafure it gave me; but ———— came in, and fome
         other

other things interrupted me; fo that
the fine vapour has evaporated—yet,
leaving a fweet fcent behind, I have
only to tell you, what is fufficiently
obvious, that the earneft defire I have
fhown to keep my place, or gain more
ground in your heart, is a fure proof
how neceffary your affeƈtion is to my
happinefs.—Still I do not think it falfe
delicacy, or foolifh pride, to wifh that
your attention to my happinefs fhould
arife *as much* from love, which is always rather a felfifh paffion, as reafon—
that is, I want you to promote my
felicity, by feeking your own.—For,
whatever pleafure it may give me to
difcover your generofity of foul, I
would not be dependent for your affeƈtion on the very quality I moft admire. No; there are qualities in your
heart, which demand my affeƈtion;
                                        but,

but, unlefs the attachment appears to me clearly mutual, I fhall labour only to efteem your character, inftead of cherifhing a tendernefs for your perfon.

I write in a hurry, becaufe the little one, who has been fleeping a long time, begins to call for me. Poor thing! when I am fad, I lament that all my affections grow on me, till they become too ftrong for my peace, though they all afford me fnatches of exquifite enjoyment—This for our little girl was at firft very reafonable—more the effect of reafon, a fenfe of duty, than feeling—now, fhe has got into my heart and imagination, and when I walk out without her, her little figure is ever dancing before me.

You too have fomehow clung round my heart—I found I could net eat my

dinner

dinner in the great room—and, when I took up the large knife to carve for myfelf, tears rufhed into my eyes.—Do not however fuppofe that I am melancholy—for, when you are from me, I not only wonder how I can find fault with you—but how I can doubt your affection.

I will not mix any comments on the inclofed (it roufed my indignation) with the effufion of tendernefs, with which I affure you, that you are the friend of my bofom, and the prop of my heart.

* * * *

LETTER

LETTER XXII.

H—, Auguſt 20.

I WANT to know what ſteps you have taken reſpecting ——. Knavery always rouſes my indignation—I ſhould be gratified to hear that the law had chaſtiſed ——— feverely; but I do not wiſh you to ſee him, becauſe the buſineſs does not now admit of peaceful difcuſſion, and I do not exactly know how you would expreſs your contempt.

Pray aſk ſome queſtions about Tallien—I am ſtill pleaſed with the dignity of his conduct.—The other day, in the cauſe of humanity, he made uſe of a degree of addreſs, which I admire—

and

and mean to point out to you, as one
of the few inftances of addrefs which
do credit to the abilities of the man,
without taking away from that confidence in his opennefs of heart, which
is the true bafis of both public and
private friendfhip.

Do not fuppofe that I mean to allude to a little referve of temper in you,
of which I have fometimes complained! You have been ufed to a
cunning woman, and you almoft look
for cunning—Nay, in *managing* my
happinefs, you now and then wounded
my fenfibility, concealing yourfelf, till
honeft fympathy, giving you to me
without difguife, lets me look into a
heart, which my half-broken one wifhes
to creep into, to be revived and
cherifhed.——You have franknefs of
heart, but not often exactly that overflowing

flowing *(épanchement de cœur)*, which becoming almoſt childiſh, appears a weakneſs only to the weak.

But I have left poor Tallien. I wanted you to enquire likewiſe whether, as a member declared in the convention, Robeſpierre really maintained a *number* of miſtreſſes.—Should it prove ſo, I ſuſpect that they rather flattered his vanity than his ſenſes.

Here is a chatting, deſultory epiſtle! But do not ſuppoſe that I mean to cloſe it without mentioning the little damſel—who has been almoſt ſpringing out of my arm—ſhe certainly looks very like you—but I do not love her the leſs for that, whether I am angry or pleaſed with you.—

Yours affectionately

＊ ＊ ＊ ＊

LETTER

LETTER XXIII*.

September 22.

I HAVE juft written two letters, that are going by other conveyances, and which I reckon on your receiving long before this. I therefore merely write, becaufe I know I fhould be difappointed at feeing any one who had left you, if you did not fend a letter, were it ever fo fhort, to tell me why you did not write a longer—and you will want to be told, over and over again, that our little Hercules is quite recovered.

* This is the firft of a feries of letters written during a feparation of many months, to which no cordial meeting ever fucceeded. They were fent from Paris, and bear the addrefs of London.

Befides

Befides looking at me, there are three other things, which delight her — to ride in a coach, to look at a fcarlet waiftcoat, and hear loud mufic—yefterday, at the *fête*, fhe enjoyed the two latter; but, to honour J. J. Rouffeau, I intend to give her a fafh, the firft fhe has ever had round her—and why not? —for I have always been half in love with him.

Well, this you will fay is trifling— fhall I talk about alum or foap? There is nothing picturefque in your prefent purfuits; my imagination then rather chufes to ramble back to the barrier with you, or to fee you coming to meet me, and my bafket of grapes.— With what pleafure do I recollect your looks and words, when I have been fitting on the window, regarding the waving corn!

Believe

Believe me, fage fir, you have not fufficient refpect for the · imagination— I could prove to you in a trice that it is the mother of fentiment, the great diftinction of our nature, the only purifier of the paffions—animals have a portion of reafon, and equal, if not more exquifite, fenfes; but no trace of imagination, or her offspring tafte, appears in any of their actions. The impulfe of the fenfes, paffions, if you will, and the conclufions of reafon, draw men together; but the imagination is the true fire, ftolen from heaven, to animate this cold creature of clay, producing all thofe fine fympathies that lead to rapture, rendering men focial by expanding their hearts, inftead of leaving them leifure to calculate how many comforts fociety affords.

If

If you call thefe obfervations romantic, a phrafe in this place which would
be tantamount to nonfenfical, I fhall
be apt to retort, that you are embruted
by trade, and the vulgar enjoyments of
life—Bring me then back your barrier-
face, or you fhall have nothing to fay
to my barrier-girl; and I fhall fly from
you, to cherifh the remembrances that
will ever be dear to me; for I am
yours truly

＊＊＊＊

LETTER

LETTER XXIV.

Evening, Sept. 23.

I HAVE been playing and laughing
with the little girl so long, that I cannot take up my pen to address you
without emotion. Pressing her to my
bosom, she looked so like you (*entre
nous*, your best looks, for I do not admire your commercial face) every nerve
seemed to vibrate to the touch, and I
began to think that there was something in the assertion of man and wife
being one—for you seemed to pervade
my whole frame, quickening the beat
of my heart, and lending me the sym-
pathetic tears you excited.

Have I any thing more to say to you?
No; not for the present—the rest is all
flown

flown away; and, indulging tendernefs for you, I cannot now complain of fome people here, who have ruffled my temper for two or three days paft.

———

Morning.

YESTERDAY B—— fent to me for my packet of letters. He called on me before; and I like him better than I did—that is, I have the fame opinion of his underftanding, but I think with you, he has more tendernefs and real delicacy of feeling with refpect to wo-men, than are commonly to be met with. His manner too of fpeaking of his little girl, about the age of mine, interefted me. I gave him a letter for my fifter, and requefted him to fee her.

I have been interrupted. Mr. ——
I fuppofe will write about bufinefs.
Public

Public affairs I do not defcant on, except to tell you that they write now
with great freedom and truth, and this
liberty of the prefs will overthrow the
Jacobins, I plainly perceive.

I hope you take care of your health.
I have got a habit of reftleffnefs at
night, which arifes, I believe, from
activity of mind; for, when I am alone,
that is, not near one to whom I can
open my heart, I fink into reveries and
trains of thinking, which agitate and
fatigue me.

This is my third letter; when am I
to hear from you? I need not tell you,
I fuppofe, that I am now writing with
fomebody in the room with me, and
—— is waiting to carry this to Mr.
——'s. I will then kifs the girl for
you, and bid you adieu.

I defired you, in one of my other
letters,

letters, to bring back to me your bar-rier-face—or that you fhould not be loved by my barrier-girl. I know that you will love her more and more, for fhe is a little affectionate, intelligent creature, with as much vivacity, I fhould think, as you could wifh for.

I was going to tell you of two or three things which difpleafe me here; but they are not of fufficient confe-quence to interrupt pleafing fenfa-tions. I have received a letter from Mr. ——. I want you to bring —— with you. Madame S—— is by me, reading a German tranflation of your letters—fhe defires me to give her love to you, on account of what you fay of the negroes.

Yours moft affectionately,

* * * *

LETTER

LETTER XXV.

Paris, Sept. 28.

I HAVE written to you three or four letters; but different caufes have prevented my fending them by the perfons who promifed to take or forward them. The inclofed is one I wrote to go by B——; yet, finding that he will not arrive, before I hope, and believe, you will have fet out on your return, I inclofe it to you, and fhall give it in charge to ——, as Mr.—— is detained, to whom I alfo gave a letter.

I cannot help being anxious to hear from you; but I fhall not harrafs you with accounts of inquietudes, or of cares that arife from peculiar circumftances.—I have had fo many little plagues

plagues here, that I have almoſt lamented that I left H——. ——, who
is at beſt a moſt helpleſs creature, is
now, on account of her pregnancy,
more trouble than uſe to me, ſo that I
ſtill continue to be almoſt a ſlave to the
child.—She indeed rewards me, for
ſhe is a ſweet little creature; for, ſet-
ting aſide a mother's fondneſs (which,
by the bye, is growing on me, her little
intelligent ſmiles ſinking into my heart),
ſhe has an aſtoniſhing degree of ſenſibility and obſervation. The other day
by B——'s child, a fine one, ſhe looked
like a little ſprite.—She is all life and
motion, and her eyes are not the eyes
of a fool—I will ſwear.

I ſlept at St. Germain's, in the very
room (if you have not forgot) in which
you preſſed me very tenderly to your
heart.—I did not forget to fold my
darling

darling to mine, with fenfations that
are almoft too facred to be alluded to.

Adieu, my love! Take care of yourfelf, if you wifh to be the protector of
your child, and the comfort of her
mother.

I have received, for you, letters from
——————. I want to hear how that
affair finifhes, though I do not know
whether I have moft contempt for his
folly or knavery.

Your own

* * * *

LETTER

LETTER XXVI.

October 1.

It is a heartlefs tafk to write letters, without knowing whether they will ever reach you.—I have given two to ——, who has been a-going, a-going, every day, for a week paft; and three others, which were written in a low-fpirited ftrain, a little querulous or fo, I have not been able to forward by the opportunities that were mentioned to me. *Tant mieux!* you will fay, and I will not fay nay; for I fhould be forry that the contents of a letter, when you are fo far away, fhould damp the plea-fure that the fight of it would afford— judging of your feelings by my own.

I juft

I juft now ftumbled on one of the kind
letters, which you wrote during your
laft abfence. You are then a dear
affectionate creature, and I will not
plague you. The letter which you
chance to receive, when the abfence is
fo long, ought to bring only tears of
tendernefs, without any bitter alloy,
into your eyes.

After your return I hope indeed,
that you will not be fo immerfed in
bufinefs, as during the laft three or
four months paft—for even money, taking into the account all the future comforts it is to procure, may be gained at
too dear a rate, if painful impreffions
are left on the mind.—Thefe impreffions were much more lively, foon after
you went away, than at prefent—for a
thoufand tender recollections efface the
melancholy traces they left on my mind
—and

—and every emotion is on the fame fide as my reafon, which always was on yours.—Separated, it would be almoft impious to dwell on real or imaginary imperfections of character.—I feel that I love you ; and, if I cannot be happy with you, I will feek it no where elfe.

My little darling grows every day more dear to me—and fhe often has a kifs, when we are alone together, which I give her for you, with all my heart.

I have been interrupted—and muft fend off my letter. The liberty of the prefs will produce a great effect here— the *cry of blood will not be vain!*—Some more monfters will perifh—and the Jacobins are conquered.—Yet I almoft fear the laft flap of the tail of the beaft.

I have had feveral trifling teazing incon-

inconveniencies here, which I fhall not now trouble you with a detail of.—I am fending —— back ; her pregnancy rendered her ufelefs. The girl I have got has more vivacity, which is better for the child.

I long to hear from you.—Bring a copy of —— and —— with you.

—— is ftill here : he is a loft man.— He really loves his wife, and is anxious about his children ; but his indifcriminate hofpitality and focial feelings have given him an inveterate habit of drinking, that deftroys his health, as well as renders his perfon difgufting.—If his wife had more fenfe, or delicacy, fhe might reftrain him: as it is, nothing will fave him.

Yours moft truly and affect onately
* * * *

LETTER

LETTER XXVII.

October 26.

My dear love, I began to wifh fo earneftly to hear from you, that the fight of your letters occafioned fuch pleafurable emotions, I was obliged to throw them afide till the little girl and I were alone together; and this faid little girl, our darling, is become a moft intelligent little creature, and as gay as a lark, and that in the morning too, which I do not find quite fo convenient. I once told you, that the fenfations before fhe was born, and when fhe is fucking, were pleafant; but they do not deferve to be compared to the emotions I feel, when fhe ftops to fmile upon

upon me, or laughs outright on meet-ing me unexpectedly in the ftreet, or after a fhort abfence. She has now the advantage of having two good nurfes, and I am at prefent able to difcharge my duty to her, without being the flave of it.

I have therefore employed and amufed myfelf fince I got rid of ——, and am making a progrefs in the language amongft other things. I have alfo made fome new acquaintance. I have almoft *charmed* a judge of the tribunal, R——, who, though I fhould not have thought it poffible, has humanity, if not *beaucoup d'efprit.* But let me tell you, if you do not make hafte back, I fhall be half in love with the author of the *Marfcil-leife,* who is a handfome man, a little too broad-faced or fo, and plays fweet-ly on the violin.

What

What do you fay to this threat?—
why, *entre nous*, I like to give way to
a fprightly vein, when writing to you,
that is, when I am pleafed with you.
" The devil," you know, is proverbi-
ally faid to be " in a good humour, when
he is pleafed." Will you not then be
a good boy, and come back quickly to
play with your girls? but I fhall not allow you to love the new-comer beft.

— — — — — —

— — — — — —

— — — — — —

— — — — — —

My heart longs for your return, my
love, and only looks for, and feeks happinefs with you; yet do not imagine
that I childifhly wifh you to come back,
before you have arranged things in
fuch a manner, that it will not be neceffary for you to leave us foon again;

or

or to make exertions which injure your conftitution.

Yours moft truly and tenderly

* * * *

P. S. You would oblige me by delivering the inclofed to Mr. ——, and pray call for an anfwer.—It is for a perfon uncomfortably fituated.

————————

LETTER XXVIII.

Dec. 26.

I HAVE been, my love, for fome days tormented by fears, that I would not allow to affume a form—I had been expecting you daily—and I heard that many veffels had been driven on fhore during the late gale.—Well, I now fee your

your letter—and find that you are fafe;
I will not regret then that your exertions have hitherto been fo unavailing.

— — — — — —
— — — — — —
— — — — — —

Be that as it may, return to me when
you have arranged the other matters,
which —— has been crowding on you.
I want to be fure that you are fafe—
and not feparated from me by a fea that
muft be paffed. For, feeling that I am
happier than I ever was, do you wonder at my fometimes dreading that fate
has not done perfecuting me? Come
to me, my deareft friend, hufband, father of my child!—All thefe fond ties
glow at my heart at this moment, and
dim my eyes.—With you an independence is defirable; and it is always
within our reach, if affluence efcapes
us

us—without you the world again appears empty to me. But I am recur-
ring to fome of the melancholy thoughts
that have flitted acrofs my mind for
fome days paft, and haunted my
dreams.

My little darling is indeed a fweet
child; and I am forry that you are not
here, to fee her little mind unfold itfelf.
You talk of " dalliance;" but certainly
no lover was ever more attached to his
miftrefs, than fhe is to me. Her eyes
follow me every where, and by affection I have the moft defpotic power
over her. She is all vivacity or foft-
nefs — yes; I love her more than I
thought I fhould. When I have been
hurt at your ftay, I have embraced her
as my only comfort—when pleafed with
you, for looking and laughing like
you; nay, I cannot, I find, long be angry

gry with you, whilft I am kiffing her for refembling you. But there would be no end to thefe details. Fold us both to your heart; for I am truly and affectionately

Yours

* * * *

LETTER XXIX.

December 28.

— — — — — — —

— — — — — — —

— — — — — — —

I do, my love, indeed fincerely fympathize with you in all your difappointments.—Yet, knowing that you are well, and think of me with affection,

tion, I only lament other difappointments, becaufe I am forry that you
fhould thus exert yourfelf in vain, and
that you are kept from me.

————, I know, urges you to ftay,
and is continually branching out into
new projects, becaufe he has the idle
defire to amafs a large fortune, rather
an immenfe one, merely to have the
credit of having made it. But we
who are governed by other motives,
ought not to be led on by him. When
we meet, we will difcufs this fubject—
You will liften to reafon, and it has
probably occurred to you, that it will
be better, in future, to purfue fome
fober plan, which may demand more
time, and ftill enable you to arrive at
the fame end. It appears to me abfurd
to wafte life in preparing to live.

Would it not now be poffible to arrange

range your bufinefs in fuch a manner as to avoid the inquietudes, of which I have had my fhare fince your departure? Is it not poffible to enter into bufinefs, as an employment neceffary to keep the faculties awake, and (to fink a little in the expreffions) the pot boiling, without fuffering what muft ever be confidered as a fecondary object, to engrofs the mind, and drive fentiment and affection out of the heart?·

I am in a hurry to give this letter to the perfon who has promifed to forward it with ———'s.. I wifh then to counteract, in fome meafure, what he he has doubtlefs recommended. moft warmly.

Stay, my friend, whilft it is *abfolutely* neceffary.—I will give you no tenderer name, though it glows at my heart,
unlefs

unlefs you come the moment the fet-
tling the *prefent* objects permit.—*I do not
confent* to your taking any other journey—or the little woman and I will be
off, the Lord knows where. But, as I
had rather owe every thing to your affection, and, I may add, to your reafon, (for this immoderate defire of
wealth, which makes ———— fo eager
to have you remain, is contrary to your
principles of action), I will not impor-
tune you.—I will only tell you, that I
long to fee you—and, being at peace
with you, I fhall be hurt, rather than
made angry, by delays.—Having fuffered fo much in life, do not be furprifed if I fometimes, when left to
myfelf, grow gloomy, and fuppofe that
it was all a dream, and that my happinefs is not to laft. I fay happinefs,
becaufe

becaufe remembrance retrenches all the dark fhades of.the picture.

My little one begins to fhow her teeth, and ufe her legs—She wants you to bear your part in the nurfing bufi‑nefs, for I am fatigued with dancing her, and yet fhe is not fatisfied—fhe wants you to thank her mother for tak‑ing fuch care of her, as you only can.

Yours truly

* * * *

LETTER XXX.

December 29.

THOUGH I fuppofe you have later intelligence, yet, as ———— has juft informed me that he has an opportuni‑

ty

ty of fending immediately to you, I
take advantage of it to inclofe you

— — — — — — —

How I hate this crooked bufinefs!
This intercourfe with the world, which
obliges one to fee the worft fide of
human nature! Why cannot you be
content with the objeƈt you had firft in
view, when you entered into this wearifome labyrinth?—I know very well
that you have imperceptibly been
drawn on; yet why does one projeƈt,
fuccefsful or abortive, only give place
to two others? Is it not fufficient to
avoid poverty?—I am contented to do
my part; and, even here, fufficient to
efcape from wretchednefs is not difficult to obtain. And, let me tell you,
I have my projeƈt alfo—and, if you do
not foon return, the little girl and I
will take care of ourfelves; we will not
accept

accept any of your cold kindnefs—your diftant civilities—no; not we.

This is but half jefting, for I am really tormented by the defire which ———— manifefts to have you remain where you are.—Yet why do I talk to you?—If he can perfuade you—let him! —for, if you are not happier with me, and your own wifhes do not make you throw afide thefe eternal projects, I am above ufing any arguments, though reafon as well as affection feems to offer them—if our affection be mutual, they will occur to you—and you will act accordingly.

Since my arrival here, I have found the German lady, of whom you have heard me fpeak. Her firft child died in the month; but fhe has another, about the age of my ————, a fine little creature. They are ftill but con-

triving

triving to live——earning their daily
bread—yet, though they are but juft
above poverty, I envy them.—She is a
tender, affectionate mother—fatigued
even by her attention.—However fhe
has an affectionate hufband in her turn,
to render her care light, and to fhare
her pleafure.

I will own to you that, feeling extreme tendernefs for my little girl, I
grow fad very often when I am playing with her, that you are not here, to
obferve with me how her mind unfolds,
and her little heart becomes attached!—
Thefe appear to me to be true pleafures—and ftill you fuffer them to efcape you, in fearch of what we may
never enjoy.—It is your own maxim to
" live in the prefent moment."—*If you
d.*—ftay, for God's fake; but tell me
the truth—if not, tell me when I may
expect

expect to see you, and let me not be always vainly looking for you, till I grow sick at heart.

Adieu! I am a little hurt.—I must take my darling to my bosom to comfort me.

* * * *

LETTER XXXI.

December 30.

SHOULD you receive three or four of the letters at once which I have written lately, do not think of Sir John Brute, for I do not mean to wife you. I only take advantage of every occasion, that one out of three of my epistles may reach your hands, and in-

form

form you that I am not of ———'s opinion, who talks till he makes me angry, of the neceſſity of your ſtaying two or three months longer. I do not like this life of continual inquietude—and, *entre nous*, I am determined to try to earn ſome money here myſelf, in order to convince you that, if you chuſe to run about the world to get a fortune, it is for yourſelf—for the little girl and I will live without your aſſiſtance, unleſs you are with us. I may be termed proud—Be it ſo—but I will never abandon certain principles of action.

The common run of men have ſuch an ignoble way of thinking, that, if they debauch their hearts, and proſtitute their perſons, following perhaps a guſt of inebriation, they ſuppoſe the wife, ſlave rather, whom they maintain,

tain, has no right to complain, and ought to receive the fultan, whenever he deigns to return, with open arms, though his have been polluted by half an hundred promifcuous amours during his abfence.

I confider fidelity and conftancy as two diftinct things; yet the former is neceffary, to give life to the other— and fuch a degree of refpect do I think due to myfelf, that, if only probity, which is a good thing in its place, brings you back, never return!—for, if a wandering of the heart, or even a caprice of the imagination detains you—there is an end of all my hopes of happinefs—I could not forgive it, if I would.

I have gotten into a melancholy mood, you perceive. You know my opinion of men in general; you know
that

that I think them fyftematic tyrants, and that it is the rareft thing in the world, to meet with a man with fufficient delicacy of feeling to govern defire. When I am thus fad, I lament that my little darling, fondly as I doat on her, is a girl.—I am forry to have a tie to a world that for me is ever fown with thorns.

You will call this an ill-humoured letter, when, in fact, it is the ftrongeft proof of affection I can give, to dread to lofe you. ——— has taken fuch pains to convince me that you muft and ought to ftay, that it has inconceivably depreffed my fpirits—You have always known my opinion—I have ever declared, that two people, who mean to live together, ought not to be long feparated.—If certain things are more neceffary to you than me—fearch

for

for them—Say but one word, and you
fhall never hear of me more.—If not—
for God's fake, let us ftruggle with
poverty—with any evil, but thefe continual inquietudes of bufinefs, which
I have been told were to laft but a few
months, though every day the end appears more diftant! This is the firft
letter in .this ftrain that I have determined to forward to you; the reft lie
by, becaufe I was unwilling to give you
pain, and I fhould not now write, if I
did not think that there would be no
conclufion to the fchemes, which demand, as I am told, your prefence.

* * * * †

† The perfon to whom the letters are addreffed,
was about this time at Ramfgate, on his return,
as he profeffed, to Paris, when he was recalled,
as it fhould feem, to London, by the further pref-
fure of bufinefs now accumulated upon him.

LETTER

LETTER XXXII.

January 9.

I JUST now received one of your hafty *notes*; for bufinefs fo entirely occupies you, that you have not time, or fufficient command of thought, to write letters. Beware! you feem to be got into a whirl of projects and fchemes, which are drawing you into a gulph, that, if it do not abforb your happinefs, will infallibly deftroy mine.

Fatigued during my youth by the moft arduous ftruggles, not only to obtain independence, but to render myfelf ufeful, not merely pleafure, for which I had the moft lively tafte, I

mean

mean the fimple pleafures that flow from
paffion and affection, efcaped me, but
the moft melancholy views of life were
impreffed by a difappointed heart on
my mind. Since I knew you, I have
been endeavouring to go back to my
former nature, and have allowed fome
time to glide away, winged with the
delight which only fpontaneous enjoyment can give.—Why have you fo
foon diffolved the charm?

I am really unable to bear the continual inquietude which your and
———'s never-ending plans produce.
This you may term want of firmnefs—
but you are miftaken—I have ftill fufficient firmnefs to purfue my principle
of action. The prefent mifery, I cannot find a fofter word to do juftice to
my feelings, appears to me unnecef-
fary

fary—and therefore I have not firmnefs to fupport it as you may think I
ought. I fhould have been content,
and ftill wifh, to retire with you to a
farm—My God! any thing, but thefe
continual anxieties—any thing but
commerce, which debafes the mind,
and roots out affection from the heart.

I do not mean to complain of fubor-
dinate inconveniences——yet I will
fimply obferve, that, led to expect
you every week, I did not make the
arrangements required by the prefent
circumftances, to procure the neceffaries of life. In order to have them,
a fervant, for that purpofe only, is indif-
penfible—The want of wood, has made
me catch the moft violent cold I ever
had ; and my head is fo difturbed by
continual coughing, that I am unable

to

to write without stopping frequently to recollect myself.——This however is one of the common evils which must be borne with——bodily pain does not touch the heart, though it fatigues the spirits.

Still as you talk of your return, even in February, doubtingly, I have determined, the moment the weather changes, to wean my child.——It is too soon for her to begin to divide sorrow!—— And as one has well said, " despair is a freeman," we will go and seek our fortune together.

This is not a caprice of the moment —for your absence has given new weight to some conclusions, that I was very reluctantly forming before you left me.——I do not chuse to be a secondary object.——If your feelings were in unison with mine, you would not sacrifice

facrifice fo much to vifionary profpects
of future advantage.

                                           * * * *

LETTER XXXIII.

Jan. 15

I was juft going to begin my letter
with the fag end of a fong, which would
only have told you, what I may as well.
fay fimply, that it is pleafant to forgive
thofe we love. I have received your
two letters, dated the 26th and 28th
of December, and my anger died away.
You can fcarcely conceive the effect
fome of your letters have produced on
me. After longing to hear from you
during a tedious interval of fufpenfe,
I have feen a fuperfcription written by
you—

you.—Promifing myfelf pleafure, and feeling emotion, I have laid it by me, till the perfon who brought it, left the room—when, behold! on opening it, I have found only half a dozen hafty lines, that have damped all the rifing affection of my foul.

Well, now for bufinefs—

— — — — — — —
— — — — — — —
— — — — — — —

My animal is well; I have not yet taught her to eat, but nature is doing the bufinefs. I gave her a cruft to af-fift the cutting of her teeth; and now fhe has two, fhe makes good ufe of them to gnaw a cruft, bifcuit, &c. You would laugh to fee her; fhe is juft like a little fquirrel; fhe will guard a cruft for two hours; and, after fixing her eye on an object for fome time, dart

on

on it with an aim as fure as a bird of
prey—nothing can equal her life and
fpirits. I fuffer from a cold; but it
does not affe{ her. Adieu! do not
forget to love us—and come foon to
tell us that you do.

＊ ＊ ＊ ＊

***

LETTER XXXIV.

Jan. 30.

FROM the purport of your laft letters, I fhould fuppofe that this will
fcarcely reach you; and I have already written fo many letters, that
you have either not received, or neg-
lefted to acknowledge, I do not find
it pleafant, or rather I have no inclination, to go over the fame ground
again.

again. If you have received them, and are still detained by new projects, it is useless for me to say any more on the subject. I have done with it for ever- yet I ought to remind you that your pecuniary interest suffers by your absence.

— — — — — — —

— — — — — — —

— — — — — — —

For my part, my head is turned giddy, by only hearing of plans to make money, and my contemptuous feelings have sometimes burst out. I therefore was glad that a violent cold gave me a pretext to stay at home, left I should have uttered unseasonable truths,

My child is well, and the spring will perhaps restore me ro myself.— I have endured many inconveniences this

this winter, which fhould I be afhamed
to mention, if they had been unavoida-
ble. "The fecondary pleafures of life,"
you fay, "are very neceffary to my comfort:" it may be fo; but I have ever
confidered them as fecondary. If therefore you accufe me of wanting the refolution neceffary to bear the *common**
evils of life; I fhould anfwer, that I
have not fafhioned my mind to fuftain
them, becaufe I would avoid them,
coft what it would——

　Adieu!　　　　　　　＊　＊　＊　＊

　* This probably alludes to fome expreffion of
the perfon to whom the letters are addreffed, in
which he treated as common evils, things upon
which the letter writer was difpofed to beftow a
different appellation.　　　　EDITOR.

LETTER

very difficult to write with any degree
of coherence.

You left me indifpofed, though you
have taken no notice of it; and the
moft fatiguing journey I ever had, con-
tributed to continue it. However, I
recovered my health; but a neglected
cold, and continual inquietude during
the laft two months, have reduced me
to a ftate of weaknefs I never before
experienced. Thofe who did not know
that the canker-worm was at work at
the core, cautioned me about fuckling
my child too long.—God preferve this
poor child, and render her happier
than her mother!

But I am wandering from my fubject:
indeed my head turns giddy, when I
think that all the confidence I have had
in the affection of others is come to this.

I did not expect this blow from you.

I have

I have done my duty to you and my child; and if I am not to have any return of affection to reward me, I have the sad consolation of knowing that I deserved a better fate. My soul is weary—I am sick at heart; and, but for this little darling, I would cease to care about a life, which is now stripped of every charm.

You see how stupid I am, uttering declamation, when I meant simply to tell you, that I consider your requesting me to come to you, as merely dictated by honour.—Indeed, I scarcely understand you.—You request me to come, and then tell me, that you have not given up all thoughts of returning to this place.

When I determined to live with you, I was only governed by affection.—I would share poverty with you, but I

turn

turn with affright from the fea of trouble on which you are entering.—I have
certain principles of action: I know
what I look for to found my happinefs
on.—It is not money.—With you I
wifhed for fufficient to procure the
comforts of life—as it is, lefs will
do. — I can ftill exert myfelf to
obtain the neceffaries of life for my
child, and fhe does not want more at
prefent.—I have two or three plans in
my head to earn our fubfiftence; for
do not fuppofe that, neglected by you,
I will lie under obligations of a pecuniary kind to you!—No; I would fooner
fubmit to menial fervice.—I wanted the
fupport of your affection—that gone,
all is over!—I did not think, when I
complained of ——'s contemptible avi-
dity to accumulate money, that he
                                would

would have dragged you into his fchemes.

I cannot write.—I inclofe a fragment of a letter, written foon after your departure, and another which tendernefs made me keep back when it was written.—You will fee then the fentiments of a calmer, though not a more determined, moment.—Do not infult me by faying, that " our being together is paramount to every other confideration!" Were it, you would not be running after a bubble, at the expence of my peace of mind.

Perhaps this is the laft letter you will ever receive from me.

       * * * *

LETTER

LETTER XXXVI.

Feb. 10.

You talk of " permanent views and future comfort"—not for me, for I am dead to hope. The inquietudes of the laſt winter have finiſhed the buſineſs, and my heart is not only broken, but my conſtitution deſtroyed. I conceive myſelf in a galloping conſumption, and the continual anxiety I feel at the thought of leaving my child, feeds the fever that nightly devours me. It is on her account that I again write to you, to conjure you, by all that you hold ſacred, to leave her here with the German lady you may have heard me mention! She has a child of the ſame age, and they may be brought up together,

gether, as I wifh her to be brought up. I fhall write more fully on the fubject. To facilitate this, I fhall give up my prefent lodgings, and go into the fame houfe. I can live much cheaper there, which is now become an object. I have had 3000 livres from ——, and I fhall take one more, to pay my fervant's wages, &c. and then I fhall endeavour to procure what I want by my own exertions. I fhall entirely give up the acquaintance of the Americans.

—— and.I have not been on good terms a long time. Yefterday he very unmanlily exulted over me, on account of your determination to ftay. I had provoked it, it is true, by fome afperities againft commerce, which have dropped from me, when we have argued about the propriety of your remaining where you are; and it is no matter, I

have

have drunk too deep of the bitter cup to care about trifles.

When you first entered into these plans, you bounded your views to the gaining of a thousand pounds. It was sufficient to have procured a farm in America, which would have been an independence. You find now that you did not know yourself, and that a certain situation in life is more necessary to you than you imagined—more necessary than an uncorrupted heart—For a year or two, you may procure yourself what you call pleasure; eating, drinking, and women; but, in the solitude of declining life, I shall be remembered with regret—I was going to say with remorse, but checked my pen.

As I have never concealed the nature of my connection with you, your reputation

tation will not fuffer. I fhall never have a confident : I am content with the approbation of my own mind ; and, if there be a fearcher of hearts, mine will not be defpifed. Reading what you have written relative to the defertion of women, I have often wondered how theory and practice could be fo different, till I recollected, that the fentiments of paffion, and the refolves of reafon, are very diftinct. As to my fifters, as you are fo continually hurried with bufinefs, you need not write to them—I fhall, when my mind is calmer. God blefs you! Adieu!

                                    * * * *

This has been fuch a period of barbarity and mifery, I ought not to complain of having my fhare. I wifh one moment that I had never heard of the cruelties

cruelties that have been practifed here, and the next envy the mothers who have been killed with their children. Surely I had fuffered enough in life, not to be curfed with a fondnefs, that burns up the vital ftream I am im-parting. You will think me mad : I would I were fo, that I could forget my mifery—fo that my head or heart would be ftill.——

────────────

LETTER XXXVII.

Feb. 19.

WHEN I firft received your letter, putting off your return to an indefinite time, I felt fo hurt, that I know not what I wrote. I am now calmer, though it was not the kind of wound

over

over which time has the quickeſt effect; on the contrary, the more I think, the ſadder I grow. Society fatigues me inexpreſſibly—So much ſo, that finding fault with every one, I have only reaſon enough, to diſcover that the fault is in myſelf. My child alone intereſts me, and, but for her, I ſhould not take any pains to recover my health.

As it is, I ſhall wean her, and try if by that ſtep (to which I feel a repugnance, for it is my only ſolace) I can get rid of my cough. Phyſicians talk much of the danger attending any complaint on the lungs, after a woman has ſuckled for ſome months. They lay a ſtreſs alſo on the neceſſity of keeping the mind tranquil—and, my God! how has mine been harraſſed! But whilſt the caprices of other women are gratified, " the wind of heaven not ſuffered

to

to vifit them too rudely," I have not found a guardian angel, in heaven or on earth, to ward off forrow or care from my bofom.

What facrifices have you not made for a woman you did not refpect!—But I will not go over this ground—I want to tell you that I do not underftand you. You fay that you have not given up all thoughts of returning here—and I know that it will be neceffary—nay, is. I cannot explain myfelf; but if you have not loft your memory, you will eafily divine my meaning. What! is our life then only to be made up of fe-parations? and am I only to return to a country, that has not merely loft all charms for me, but for which I feel a repugnance that almoft amounts to horror, only to be left there a prey to it!

Why

Why is it fo neceffary that I fhould return?—brought up here, my girl would be freer. Indeed, expecting you to join us, I had formed fome plans of ufefulnefs that have now vanifh-ed with my hopes of happinefs.

In the bitternefs of my heart, I could complain with reafon, that I am left here dependent on a man, whofe avi-dity to acquire a fortune has rendered him callous to every fentiment con-nected with focial or affectionate emo-tions.—With a brutal infenfibility, he cannot help difplaying the pleafure your determination to ftay gives him, in fpite of the effect it is vifible it has had on me.

Till I can earn money, I fhall en-deavour to borrow fome, for I want to avoid afking him continually for the fum neceffary to maintain me.—Do not miftake

miſtake me, I have never been refuſed.
—Yet I have gone half a dozen times
to the houſe to aſk for it, and come
away without ſpeaking——you muſt
guefs why—Beſides, I wiſh to avoid
hearing of the eternal projeɕts to which
you have ſacrificed my peace—not re-
membering—but I will be ſilent for
ever.——

————————————

LETTER XXXVIII.

April 7.

HERE I am at H——, on the wing
towards you, and I write now, only to
tell you, that you may expeɕt me in
the courfe of three or four days; for
I ſhall

I shall not attempt to give vent to the different emotions which agitate my heart—You may term a feeling, which appears to me to be a degree of delicacy that naturally arises from sensibility, pride—Still I cannot indulge the very affectionate tenderness which glows in my bosom, without trembling, till I see, by your eyes, that it is mutual.

I sit, lost in thought, looking at the sea—and tears rush into my eyes, when I find that I am cherishing any fond expectations.—I have indeed been so unhappy this winter, I find it as difficult to acquire fresh hopes, as to regain tranquillity.—Enough of this—lie still, foolish heart!—But for the little girl, I could almost wish that it should cease to beat, to be no more alive to the anguish of disappointment.

Sweet

Sweet little creature! I deprived myfelf of my only pleafure, when I weaned her, about ten days ago.—I am however glad I conquered my repugnance.
—It was neceffary it fhould be done
foon, and I did not wifh to embitter
the renewal of your acquaintance with
her, by putting it off till we met.—It
was a painful exertion to me, and I
thought it beft to throw this inquietude
with the reft, into the fack that I
would fain throw over my fhoulder.—
I wifhed to endure it alone, in fhort—
Yet, after fending her to fleep in the
next room for three or four nights, you
cannot think with what joy I took her
back again to fleep in my bofom!

I fuppofe I fhall find you, when I arrive, for I do not fee any neceffity for
your coming to me.—Pray inform Mr.
———, that I have his little friend
with

with me.—My wifhing to oblige him,
made me put myfelf to fome incon-
venience——and delay my departure;
which was irkfome to me, who have
not quite as much philofophy, I would
not for the world fay indifference, as
you. God blefs you!

Yours truly,

✱ ✱ ✱ ✱

LETTER XXXIX.

Brighthelmftone, Saturday, April 11.

HERE we are, my love, and mean to
fet out early in the morning; and, if I
can find you, I hope to dine with you
to-morrow.—I fhall drive to ———'s
hotel, where ——— tells me you have
been—

been—and, if you have left it, I hope you will take care to be there to receive us.

I have brought with me Mr. ——'s little friend, and a girl whom I like to take care of our little darling—not on the way, for that fell to my ſhare.—But why do I write about trifles?—or any thing? —Are we not to meet ſoon?—What does your heart ſay!

Yours truly

* * * *

I have weaned my ——, and ſhe is now eating away at the white bread.

LETTER

L E T T E R XL.

London, Friday, May 22.

I HAVE juft received your affectionate letter, and am diftreffed to think that I have added to your embarraffments at this troublefome juncture, when the exertion of all the faculties of your mind appears to be neceffary, to extricate you out of your pecuniary difficulties. I fuppofe it was fomething relative to the circumftance you have mentioned, which made ——— requeft to fee me to-day, to *converfe about a matter of great importance.* Be that as it may, his letter (fuch is the ftate of my fpirits) inconceivably alarmed me, and rendered

the.

the laſt night as diſtreſſing, as the two former had been.

I have laboured to calm my mind ſince you left me—Still I find that tranquillity is not to be obtained by exertion ; it is a feeling ſo different from the reſignation of deſpair!—I am however no longer angry with you—nor will I ever utter another complaint—there are arguments which convince the reaſon, whilſt they carry death to the heart.— We have had too many cruel explananations, that not only cloud every future proſpect; but embitter the remembrances which alone give life to affection.—Let the ſubject never be revived!

It ſeems to me that I have not only loſt the hope, but the power of being happy.—Every emotion is now ſharpened

ened by anguiſh.—My ſoul has been
ſhook, and my tone of feelings deſtroyed.—I have gone out—and ſought
for diſſipation, if not amuſement, merely to fatigue ſtill more, I find, my irrit-
able nerves——

My friend—my dear friend—examine yourſelf well—I am out of the
queſtion ; for, alas! I am nothing—
and diſcover what you wiſh to do—
what will render you moſt comfortable
—or, to be more explicit—whether
you deſire to live with me, or part for
ever? When you can once aſcertain it,
tell me frankly, I conjure you!—for, be
lieve me, I have very involuntarily interrupted your peace.

I ſhall expect you to dinner on Monday, and will endeavour to aſſume a
cheerful face to greet you—at any
rate

rate I will avoid converfations, which only tend to harrafs your feelings, becaufe I am moft affectionately yours,

* * * *

———

LETTER XLI.

Wednefday.

I inclose you the letter, which you defired me to forward, and I am tempted very laconically to wifh you a good morning—not becaufe I am angry, or have nothing to fay; but to keep down a wounded fpirit.—I fhall make every effort to calm my mind—yet a ftrong conviction feems to whirl round in the very centre of my brain, which, like the

LETTER XXXV.

February 9.

THE melancholy prefentiment has for fome time hung on my fpirits, that we were parted for ever; and the letters I received this day, by Mr. ——, convince me that it was not without foundation. You allude to fome other letters, which I fuppofe have mifcarried ; for moft of thofe I have got, were only a few hafty lines, calculated to wound the tendernefs the fight of the fuperfcriptions excited.

I mean not however to complain; yet fo many feelings are ftruggling for utterance, and agitating a heart almoft burfting with anguifh, that I find it

very

the fiat of fate, emphatically aſſures me, that grief has a firm hold of my heart.

God bleſs you!

Yours ſincerely

* * * ●

––––––––––––

L E T T E R XLII.

—, Wedneſday, Two o'Clock.

WE arrived here about an hour ago. I am extremely fatigued with the child, who would not reſt quiet with any body but me, during the night—and now we are here in a comfortleſs, damp room, in a ſort of a tomb-like houſe. This however I ſhall quickly remedy,

remedy, for, when I have finished this letter, (which I muſt do immediately, becauſe the poſt goes out early), I ſhall ſally forth, and enquire about a veſſel and an inn.

I will not diſtreſs you by talking of the depreſſion of my ſpirits, or the ſtruggle I had to keep alive my dying heart.—It is even now too full to allow me to write with compoſure.—*****, —dear *****, —am I always to be toſſed about thus?—ſhall I never find an aſylum to reſt *contented* in? How can you love to fly about continually— dropping down, as it were, in a new world—cold and ſtrange!—every other day? Why do you not attach thoſe tender emotions round the idea of home, which even now dim my eyes?—This alone is affection—every thing elſe is only humanity, electrified by ſympathy.

I will

I will write to you again to-morrow, when I know how long I am to be detained—and hope to get a letter quickly from you, to cheer yours sincerely and affectionately

* * * *

———— is playing near me in high spirits. She was so pleased with the noise of the mail-horn, she has been continually imitating it.——Adieu!

LETTER XLIII.

Thursday.

A LADY has just sent to offer to take me to ————. I have then only a moment to exclaim against the vague manner

manner in which people give information   —   —   —   —   —

—   —   —   —   —   —

—   —   —   —   —   —

—   —   —   —   —   —

—   —   —   —   —   —

But why talk of inconveniences, which
are in fact trifling, when compared
with the finking of the heart I have
felt! I did not intend to touch this
painful ftring—God blefs you!

Yours truly,

* * * *

LETTER

LETTER XLIV.

Friday, June 12.

I HAVE juſt received yours dated the 9th, which I ſuppoſe was a miſtake, for it could ſcarcely have loitered ſo long on the road. The general obſervations which apply to the ſtate of your own mind, appear to me juſt, as far as they go; and I ſhall always conſider it as one of the moſt ſerious misfortunes of my life, that I did not meet you, before ſatiety had rendered your ſenſes ſo faſtidious, as almoſt to cloſe up every tender avenue of ſentiment and affection that leads to your ſympathetic heart. You have a heart, my friend, yet, hurried away by the impetuoſity of inferior feelings, you have ſought in vulgar exceſſes,

excesses, for that gratification which only the heart can bestow.

The common run of men, I know, with strong health and grofs appetites, must have variety to banifh *ennui*, becaufe the imagination never lends its magic wand, to convert appetite into love, cemented by according reafon.—— Ah! my friend, you know not the ineffable delight, the exquifite pleafure, which arifes from a unifon of affection and defire, when the whole foul and fenfes are abandoned to a lively imagination, that renders every emotion delicate and rapturous. Yes; thefe are emotions, over which fatiety has no power, and the recollection of which, even difappointment cannot difenchant; but they do not exift without felf-denial. Thefe emotions, more or lefs ftrong, appear to me to be the diftinctive

tive characteriftic of genius, the foundation of tafte, and of that exquifite
relifh for the beauties of nature, of
which the common herd of eaters and
drinkers and *child-begeters*, certainly
have no idea. You will fmile at an
obfervation that has juft occurred to me:
—I confider thofe minds as the moft
ftrong and original, whofe imagination
acts as the ftimulus to their fenfes.

Well! you will afk, what is the refult of all this reafoning? Why I cannot help thinking that it is poffible for
you, having great ftrength of mind,
to return to nature, and regain a fanity
of conftitution, and purity of feeling—
which would open your heart to me.—
I would fain reft there!

Yet, convinced more than ever of
the fincerity and tendernefs of my attachment to you, the involuntary hopes,
which

which a determination to live has revived, are not fufficiently ftrong to diffipate the cloud, that defpair has fpread
over futurity. I have looked at the
fea, and at my child, hardly daring to
own to myfelf the fecret wifh, that it
might become our tomb; and that the
heart, ftill fo alive to anguifh, might
there be quieted by death. At this
moment ten thoufand complicated fentiments prefs for utterance, weigh on
my heart, and obfcure my fight.

Are we ever to meet again? and will
you endeavour to render that meeting
happier than the laft? Will you endeavour to reftrain your caprices, in order
to give vigour to affeΕtion, and to give
play to the checked fentiments that
nature intended fhould expand your
heart? I cannot indeed, without agony, think of your bofom's being continually

nually contaminated; and bitter are
the tears which exhauft my eyes, when
I recollect why my child and I are
forced to ftray from the afylum, in
which, after fo many ftorms, I had
hoped to reft, fmiling at angry fate.
—Thefe are not common forrows; nor
can you perhaps conceive, how much
active fortitude it requires to labour
perpetually to blunt the fhafts of difappointment.

Examine now yourfelf, and afcer-
tain whether you can live in fomething-
like a fettled ftile. Let our confidence
in future be unbounded; confider whether you find it neceffary to facrifice
me to what you term " the zeft of life;"
and, when you have once a clear view
of your own motives, of your own in-
centive to action, do not deceive me!

The train of thoughts which the
writing

writing of this epiftle awoke, makes me fo wretched, that I muft take a walk, to roufe and calm my mind. But firft, let me tell you, that, if you really wifh to promote my happinefs, you will endeavour to give me as much as you can of yourfelf. You have great mental energy; and your judgment feems to me fo juft, that it is only the dupe of your inclination in difcuffing one fubject.

The poft does not go out to-day. To-morrow I may write more tranquilly. I cannot yet fay when the veffel will fail in which I have determined to depart.

———

Saturday Morning.

Your fecond letter reached me about an hour ago. You were certainly wrong

wrong, in fuppofing that I did not mention you with refpect; though, without
my being confcious of it, fome fparks
of refentment may have animated the
gloom of defpair—Yes; with lefs affection, I fhould have been more refpectful. However the regard which I
have for you, is fo unequivocal to myfelf, I imagine that it muft be fufficiently obvious to every body elfe. Befides, the only letter I intended for the
public eye was to ——, and that I deftroyed from delicacy before you faw
them, becaufe it was only written (of
courfe warmly in your praife) to prevent any odium being thrown on you*.

I am harraffed by your embarraffments, and fhall certainly ufe all my

* This paffage refers to letters written under
a purpofe of fuicide, and not intended to be
opened till after the cataftrophe.

efforts,

efforts, to make the bufinefs terminate to your fatisfaction in which I am engaged.

My friend—my deareft friend—I feel my fate united to yours by the moft facred principles of my foul, and the yearns of—yes, I will fay it—a true, unfophifticated heart.

Yours moft truly

* * « *

If the wind be fair, the captain talks of failing on Monday; but I am afraid I fhall be detained fome days longer. At any rate, continue to write, (I want this fupport) till you are fure I am where I cannot expect a letter; and, if any fhould arrive after my departure, a gentleman (not Mr. ——'s friend, I promife you) from whom I

have

have received great civilities, will fend
them after me.

Do write by every occafion! I am
anxious to hear how your affairs go on;
and, ftill more, to be convinced that you
are not feparating yourfelf from us.
For my little darling is calling papa,
and adding her parrot word—Come,
Come! And will you not come, and
let us exert ourfelves?—I fhall recover
all my energy, when I am convinced
that my exertions will draw us more
clofely together. One more adieu!

LETTER

LETTER XLV.

Sunday, June 14.

I RATHER expected to hear from you to-day—I wifh you would not fail to write to me for a little time, becaufe I am not quite well—Whether I have any good fleep or not, I wake in the morning in violent fits of trembling—and, in fpite of all my efforts, the child— every thing—fatigues me, in which I feek for folace or amufement,

Mr. —— forced on me a letter to a phyfician of this place; it was fortunate, for I fhould otherwife have had fome difficulty to obtain the neceffary information. His wife is a pretty woman (I can admire, you know, a pretty woman,

man, when I am alone) and he an intelligent and rather interesting man.—
They have behaved to me with great
hospitality; and poor ———— was never
so happy in her life, as amongst their
young brood.

They took me in their carriage to
——————, and I ran over my favourite
walks, with a vivacity that would have
astonished you.——The town did not
please me quite so well as formerly——
It appeared so diminutive; and, when
I found that many of the inhabitants
had lived in the same houses ever since
I left it, I could not help wondering
how they could thus have vegetated,
whilst I was running over a world of
sorrow, snatching at pleasure, and
throwing off prejudices. The place
where I at present am, is much improved; but it is astonishing what
strides

ſtrides ariſtocracy and fanaticiſm have made, ſince I reſided in this country.

The wind does not appear inclined to change, ſo I am ſtill forced to linger —When do you think that you ſhall be able to ſet out for France? I do not entirely like the aſpect of your affairs, and ſtill leſs your connections on either ſide of the water. Often do I ſigh, when I think of your entanglements in buſineſs, and your extreme reſtleſſneſs of mind.—Even now I am almoſt afraid to aſk you, whether the pleaſure of being free, does not over-balance the pain you felt at parting with me? Sometimes I indulge the hope that you will feel me neceſſary to you—or why ſhould we meet again?—but, the moment after, deſpair damps my riſing ſpirits, aggravated by the
emotions

emotions of tendernefs, which ought to foften the cares of life.——God blefs you!

Yours fincerely and affectionately

* * * *

———————

LETTER XLVI.

June 15.

I WANT to know how you have fettled with refpect to ————. In fhort, be very particular in your account of all your affairs—let our confidence, my dear, be unbounded.— The laft time we were feparated, was a feparation indeed on your part— Now you have acted more ingenuoufly.

let

let the moft affectionate interchange of
fentiments fill up the aching void of
difappointment.   I almoft dread that
your plans will prove abortive—yet
fhould the moft unlucky turn fend
you home to us, convinced that a true
friend is a treafure, I fhould not much
mind having to ftruggle with the world
again.   Accufe me not of pride—yet
fometimes, when nature has opened
my heart to its author, I have wondered
that you did not fet a higher value on
my heart.

Receive a kifs from ————, I was
going to add, if you will not take one
from me, and believe me yours

Sincerely

* * * *

The wind ftill continues in the fame
quarter.

LETTER

LETTER XLVII.

Tuefday Morning.

THE captain has juft fent to inform me, that I muft be on board in the courfe of a few hours.—I wifhed to have ftayed till to-morrow. It would have been a comfort to me to have received another letter from you—Should one arrive, it will be fent after me.

My fpirits are agitated, I fcarcely know why——The quitting England feems to be a frefh parting.—Surely you will not forget me.—A thoufand weak forebodings affault my foul, and the ftate of my health renders me fenfible to every thing. It is furprifing that in London, in a continual con-

fli&

flict of mind, I was still growing better—whilst here, bowed down by the
despotic hand of fate, forced into re-
signation by despair, I seem to be fading away—perishing beneath a cruel
blight, that withers up all my faculties.

The child is perfectly well. My
hand seems unwilling to add adieu! I
know not why this inexpressible sad-
ness has taken possession of me.—It is
not a presentiment of ill. Yet, having
been so perpetually the sport of disappointment,—having a heart that has
been as it were a mark for misery, I
dread to meet wretchedness in some
new shape.—Well, let it come—I care
not!—what have I to dread, who have
so little to hope for! God bless you—
I am most affectionately and sincerely
yours

                     * * * *

             LETTER

LETTER XLVIII.

Wednesday Morning.

I was hurried on board yesterday about three o'clock, the wind having changed. But before evening it veered round to the old point; and here we are, in the midst of mists and water, only taking advantage of the tide to advance a few miles.

You will scarcely suppose that I left the town with reluctance—yet it was even so—for I wished to receive another letter from you, and I felt pain at parting, for ever perhaps, from the amiable family, who had treated me with so much hospitality and kindness. They will probably send me your letter, if it arrives

arrives this morning; for here we are likely to remain, I am afraid to think how long.

The veffel is very commodious, and the captain a civil, open-hearted kind of man. There being no other paffengers, I have the cabin to myfelf, which is pleafant; and I have brought a few books with me to beguile wearinefs; but I feem inclined, rather to employ the dead moments of fufpence in writing fome effufions, than in reading.

What are you about? How are your affairs going on? It may be a long time before you anfwer thefe queftions. My dear friend, my heart finks within me!—Why am I forced thus to ftruggle continually with my affections and feelings?—Ah! why are thofe affections and feelings the fource

of

of fo much mifery, when they feem to have been given to vivify my heart, and extend my ufefulnefs! But I muft not dwell on this fubjeft.—Will you not endeavour to cherifh all the affeftion you can for me? What am I faying? —Rather forget me, if you can—if other gratifications are dearer to you!—How is every remembrance of mine embittered by difappointment? What a world is this!—They only feem happy, who never look beyond fenfual or artificial enjoyments.—Adieu!

———— begins to play with the cabin-boy, and is as gay as a lark.—I will labour to be tranquil; and am in every mood,

Yours fincerely

* * * *

LETTER

LETTER XLIX.

Thurſday.

HERE I am ſtill—and I have juſt received your letter of Monday by the
pilot, who promiſed to bring it to me,
if we were detained, as he expected,
by the wind.—It is indeed weariſome
to be thus toſſed about without going forward.—I have a violent head-
ache—yet I am obliged to take care of
the child, who is a little tormented
by her teeth, becauſe ———— is unable to do any thing, ſhe is rendered
ſo ſick by the motion of the ſhip, as
we ride at anchor.

Theſe are however trifling inconveniences, compared with anguiſh of
mind—compared with the ſinking of a
broken

broken heart.—To tell you the truth, I never fuffered in my life fo much from depreffion of fpirits—from defpair.—I do not fleep—or, if I clofe my eyes, it is to have the moft terrifying dreams, in which I often meet you with different cafts of countenance..

I will not, my dear ———, torment you by dwelling on my fufferings—and will ufe all my efforts to calm my mind, inftead of deadening it—at prefent it is moft painfully active. I find I am not equal to thefe continual ftruggles—yet your letter this morning has afforded me fome comfort—and I will try to revive hope. One thing let me tell you— when we meet again—furely we are to meet!—it muft be to part no more. I mean not to have feas between us—it is more than I can fupport..

The

The pilot is hurrying me—God blefs you.

In fpite of the commodioufnefs of the veffel, every thing here would dif-guft my fenfes, had I nothing elfe to think of—" When the mind's free, the body's delicate;"—mine has been too much hurt to regard trifles.

Yours mofl truly

* *, *, *,

———————

LETTER L.

Saturday.

THIS is the fifth dreary day I have been imprifoned by the wind, with every outward objeƈt to difguft the fenfes, and unable to banifh the re-membrances that fadden my heart.

How

How am I altered by difappointment!—When going to ——, ten years
ago, the elafticity of my mind was
fufficient to ward off wearinefs—and
the imagination ftill could dip her
brufh in the rainbow of fancy, and
fketch futurity in fmiling colours. Now
I am going towards the North in
fearch of funbeams!—Will any ever
warm this defolated heart? All nature
feems to frown—or rather mourn with
me.—Every thing is cold—cold as my
expectations! Before I left the fhore,
tormented, as I now am, by thefe
North eaft *chillers*, I could not help
exclaiming—Give me, gracious Heaven! at leaft, genial weather, if I am
never to meet the genial affection that
ftill warms this agitated bofom—com-
pelling life to linger there.

I am now going on fhore with the
captain,

captain, though the weather be rough,
to feek for milk, &c. at a little village,
and to take a walk—after which I hope
to fleep—for, confined here, furrounded by difagreeable fmells, I have loft
the little appetite I had; and I lie
awake, till thinking almoft drives me
to the brink of madnefs—only to the
brink, for I never forget, even in the
feverifh flumbers I fometimes fall into,
the mifery I am labouring to blunt the
the fenfe of, by every exertion in my
power.

Poor ———— ftill continues fick,
and ———— grows weary when the
weather will not allow her to remain
on deck.

I hope this will be the laft letter I fhall
write from England to you—are you
not tired of this lingering adieu?

Yours truly

* * * *

LETTER

LETTER LI.

Sunday Morning.

THE captain laft night, after I had written my letter to you intended to be left at a little village, offered to go to —— to pafs to-day. We had a troublefome fail—and now I muft hurry on board again, for the wind has changed.

I half expected to find a letter from you here. Had you written one haphazard, it would have been kind and confiderate—you might have known, had you thought, that the wind would not permit me to depart. Thefe are attentions, more grateful to the heart than

than offers of fervice—But why do I foolifhly continue to look for them?

Adieu! adieu! My friend—your friendfhip is very cold—you fee I am hurt.—God blefs you! I may perhaps be, fome time or other, independent in every fenfe of the word—Ah! there is but one fenfe of it cf confequence. I will break or bend this weak heart— yet even now it is full.

Yours fincerely

* * * *

The child is well; I did not leave her on board.

LETTER

LETTER LII.

June 27, Saturday.

I ARRIVED in ———— this afternoon, after vainly attempting to land
at ————. I have now but a moment,
before the post goes out, to inform you
we have got here; though not without
confiderable difficulty, for we were fet
afhore in a boat above twenty miles
below.

What I fuffered in the veffel I will
not now defcant upon—nor mention
the pleafure I received from the fight
of the rocky coaft.—This morning
however, walking to join the carriage
that was to tranfport us to this place,
I fell

I fell, without any previous warning, fenfelefs on the rocks—and how I efcaped with life I can fcarcely guefs. I was in a ftupour for a quarter of an hour; the fuffufion of blood at laft reftored me to my fenfes—the contufion is great, and my brain confufed. The child is well.

Twenty miles ride in the rain, after my accident, has fufficiently deranged me—and here I could not get a fire to warm me, or any thing warm to eat; the inns are mere ftables—I muft neverthelefs go to bed. For God's fake, let me hear from you immediately, my friend! I am not well, and yet you fee I cannot die.

Yours fincerely

* * * *

LETTER

LETTER LIII.

June 29.

I WROTE to you by the laſt poſt, to inform you of my arrival; and I believe I alluded to the extreme fatigue I endured on ſhip-board, owing to———'s illneſs, and the roughneſs of the weather—I likewiſe mentioned to you my fall, the effects of which I ſtill feel, though I do not think it will have any ſerious conſequences.

——— will go with me, if I find it neceſſary to go to ———. The inns here are ſo bad, I was forced to accept of an apartment in his houſe. I am overwhelmed with civilities on all ſides, and

and fatigued with the endeavours to amuſe me, from which I cannot eſcape.

My friend—my friend, I am not well—a deadly weight of ſorrow lies heavily on my heart. I am again toſſed on the troubled billows of life; and obliged to cope with difficulties, without being buoyed up by the hopes that alone render them bearable. " How flat, dull, and unprofitable," appears to me all the buſtle into which I ſee people here ſo eagerly enter! I long every night to go to bed, to hide my melancholy face in my pillow; but there is a canker-worm in my boſom that never ſleeps.

* * * *

LETTER

LETTER LIV.

July 1.

I LABOUR in vain to calm my mind—my foul has been overwhelmed by forrow and difappointment. Every thing fatigues me—this is a life that cannot laft long. It is you who muft determine with refpect to futurity—and, when you have, I will act accordingly—I mean, we muft either refolve to live together, or part for ever, I cannot bear thefe continual ftruggles—But I wifh you to examine carefully your own heart and mind; and, if you perceive the leaft chance of being happier without me than with me, or if your inclination

nation leans capriciously to that side, do not dissemble ; but tell me frankly that you will never see me more. I will then adopt the plan I mentioned to you—for we must either live together, or I will be entirely independent.

My heart is so oppressed, I cannot write with precision—You know however that what I so imperfectly express, are not the crude sentiments of the moment—You can only contribute to my comfort (it is the consolation I am in need of) by being with me—and, if the tenderest friendship is of any value, why will you not look to me for a degree of satisfaction that heartless affections cannot bestow ?

Tell me then, will you determine to meet me at Basle ?—I shall, I should imagine, be at —— before the close of August ; and, after you settle your affairs

affairs at Paris, could we not meet there?

God blefs you!

Yours truly

* * * *

Poor ———— has fuffered during the journey with her teeth.

———————————

L E T T E R LV.

July 3.

THERE was a gloominefs diffufed through your laft letter, the impreffion of which ftill refts on my mind—though, recollecting how quickly you throw off the forcible feelings of the moment, I flatter

flatter myfelf it has long fince given
place to your ufual cheerfulnefs.

Believe me (and my eyes fill with
tears of tendernefs as I affure you)
there is nothing I would not endure in
the way of privation, rather than dif-
turb your tranquillity.—If I am fated
to be unhappy, I will labour to hide
my forrows in my own bofom; and you
fhall always find me a faithful, affectionate friend.

I grow more and more attached to
my little girl—and I cherifh this affection without fear, becaufe it muft be
a long time before it can become bitternefs of foul.—She is an interefting
creature.—On fhip-board, how often
as I gazed at the fea, have I longed to
bury my troubled bofom in the lefs
troubled deep; afferting with Brutus,
" that the virtue I had followed too
far,

far, was merely an empty name!" and nothing but the fight of her—her playful fmiles, which feemed to cling and twine round my heart—could have ftopped me.

What peculiar mifery has fallen to my fhare! To act up to my princi- ples, I have laid the ftricteft reftraint on my very thoughts—yes; not to fully the delicacy of my feelings, I have reined in my imagination; and ftart- ed with affright from every fenfation, (I allude to ——) that ftealing with balmy fweetnefs into my foul, led me to fcent from afar the fragrance of re- viving nature.

My friend, I have dearly paid for one conviction.—Love, in fome minds, is an affair of fentiment, arifing from the fame delicacy of perception (or tafte) as renders them alive to the
beauties

beauties of nature, poetry, &c, alive to the charms of thofe evanefcent graces that are, as it were, impalpable—they muft be felt, they cannot be defcribed.

Love is a want of my heart. I have examined myfelf lately with more care than formerly, and find, that to deaden is not to calm the mind—Aiming at tranquillity, I have almoft deftroyed all the energy of my foul—almoft rooted out what renders it eftimable—Yes, I have damped that enthufiafm of cha- racter, which converts the groffeft materials into a fuel, that impercep- tibly feeds hopes, which afpire above common enjoyment. Defpair, fince the birth of my child, has rendered me ftupid—foul and body feemed to be fading away before the withering touch of difappointment.

I am

I am now endeavouring to recover myfelf—and fuch is the elafticity of my conftitution, and the purity of the atmofphere here, that health unfought for, begins to reanimate my countenance.

I have the fincereft efteem and affection for you—but the defire of regaining peace, (do you underftand me?) has made me forget the refpect due to my own emotions—facred emotions, that are the fure harbingers of the delights I was formed to enjoy——and fhall enjoy, for nothing can extinguifh the heavenly fpark.

Still, when we meet again, I will not torment you, I promife you. I blufh when I recollect my former conduct—and will not in future confound myfelf with the beings whom I feel to be be my inferiors.—I will liften to deli-cacy, or pride.

LETTER LVI.

July 4.

I HOPE to hear from you by to-mor-row's mail. My deareft friend! I can-not tear my affections from you—and, though every remembrance ftings me to the foul, I think of you, till I make allowance for the very defects of cha-racter, that have given fuch a cruel ftab to my peace.

Still however I am more alive, than you have feen me for a long, long time.

I have

I have a degree of vivacity, even in my grief, which is preferable to the benumbing ftupour that, for the laft year, has frozen up all my faculties.—Perhaps this change is more owing to returning health, than to the vigour of my reafon—for, in fpite of fadnefs (and furely I have had my fhare), the purity of this air, and the being continually out in it, for I fleep in the country every night, has made an alteration in my appearance that really furprifes me.— The rofy fingers of health already ftreak my cheeks—and I have feen a *phyfical* life in my eyes, after I have been climbing the rocks, that refembled the fond, credulous hopes of youth.

With what a cruel figh have I recollected that I had forgotten to hope!— Reafon, or rather experience, does not thus cruelly damp poor ———'s pleafures;

fures; fhe plays all day in the garden with ————'s children, and makes friends for heifelf.

Do not tell me, that you are happier without us—Will you not come to us in Switzerland? Ah, why do not you love us with more fentiment?—why are you a creature of fuch fympathy, that the warmth of your feelings, or rather quicknefs of your fenfes, hardens your heart? It is my misfortune, that my imagination is perpetually fhading your defects, and lending you charms, whilft the groffnefs of your fenfes makes you (call me not vain) overlook graces in me, that only dignity of mind, and the fenfibility of an expanded heart can give.—God blefs you! Adieu.

LETTER

LETTER LVII.

July 7.

I COULD not help feeling extremely mortified laft poft, at not receiving a letter from you. My being at ———— was but a chance, and you might have hazarded it; and would a year ago.

I fhall not however complain— There are misfortunes fo great, as to filence the ufual expreffions of forrow— Believe me, there is fuch a thing as a broken heart! There are characters whofe very energy preys upon them; and who, ever inclined to cherifh by reflection fome paffion, cannot reft fatisfied with the common comforts of life.

life. I have endeavoured to fly from myfelf, and launched into all the diffipation poffible here, only to feel keener anguifh, when alone with my child.

Still, could any thing pleafe me—had not difappointment cut me off from life, this romantic country, thefe fine evenings, would intereft me.—My God! can any thing? and am I ever to feel alive only to painful fenfations?—But it cannot—it fhall not laft long.

The poft is again arrived; I have fent to feek for letters, only to be wounded to the foul by a negative.—My brain feems on fire. I muft go into the air.

* * * *

LETTER

LETTER LVIII.

July 14.

I AM now on my journey to ———.
I felt more at leaving my child, than I
thought I fhould—and, whilft at night
I imagined every inftant that I heard
the half-formed founds of her voice,—
I afked myfelf how I could think of
parting with her for ever, of leaving
her thus helplefs?

Poor lamb! It may run very well
in a tale, that " God will temper the
winds to the fhorn lamb!" but how
can I expect that fhe will be fhielded,
when my naked bofom has had to
brave continually the pitilefs ftorm?
Yes;

Yes; I could add, with poor Lear—
What is the war of elements to the
pangs of difappointed affection, and
the horror arifing from a difcovery of
a breach of confidence, that fnaps every
focial tie!

All is not right fomewhere!—When
you firft knew me, I was not thus loft.
I could ftill confide—for I opened my
heart to you—of this only comfort you
have deprived me, whilft my happinefs, you tell me, was your firft object.
Strange want of judgment!

I will not complain; but, from the
foundnefs of your underftanding, I am
convinced, if you give yourfelf leave to
reflect, you will alfo feel, that your
conduct to me, fo far from being generous, has not been juft.—I mean not
to allude to factitious principles of
morality; but to the fimple bafis of all
                              rectitude.

rectitude.—However I did not intend to argue—Your not writing is cruel —and my reaſon is perhaps diſturbed by conſtant wretchednefs.

Poor ——— would fain have accompanied me, out of tendernefs; for my fainting, or rather convulſion, when I landed, and my ſudden changes of countenance ſince, have alarmed her ſo much, that ſhe is perpetually afraid of ſome accident—But it would have injured the child this warm ſeaſon, as ſhe is cutting her teeth.

I hear not of your having written to me at ———. Very well! Act as you pleafe—there is nothing I fear or care for! When I ſee whether I can, or cannot obtain the money I am come here about, I will not trouble you with letters to which you do not reply.

LETTER

LETTER LIX.

July 18.

I ᴀᴍ here in ———, feparated from my child—and here I muft remain a month at leaft, or I might as well never have come. — — —
— — — — — —
— — — — — —
— — — — — —

I have begun ————— which will, I hope, difcharge all my obligations of a pecuniary kind.—I am lowered in my own eyes, on account of my not having done it fooner.

I fhall make no further comments on your filence.   God blefs you!

* * * *

LETTER

LETTER LX.

July 30.

I HAVE juſt received two of your letters, dated the 26th and 30th of June; and you muſt have received ſeveral from me, informing you of my detention, and how much I was hurt by your ſilence.

— — — — — — —

— — — — — — —

— — — — — — —

Write to me then, my friend, and write explicitly. I have ſuffered, God knows, ſince I left you. Ah! you have never felt this kind of ſickneſs of heart! —My mind however is at preſent painfully active, and the ſympathy I feel

feel almoſt riſes to agony. But this is not a ſubjeɛt of complaint, it has afforded me pleaſure,——and reflcɛted pleaſure is all I have to hope for—if a ſpark of hope be yet alive in my forlorn boſom.

I will try to write with a degree of compoſure. I wiſh for us to live together, becauſe I want you to acquire an habitual tenderneſs for my poor girl. I cannot bear to think of leaving her alone in the world, or that ſhe ſhould only be protecɛted by your ſenſe of duty. Next to preſerving her, my moſt earneſt wiſh is not to diſturb your peace. I have nothing to expeɛt, and little to fear, in life—There are wounds that can never be healed—but they may be allowed to feſter in ſilence without wincing.

When we meet again, you ſhall be convinced

convinced that I have more refolution than you give me credit for. I will not torment you. If I am deftined always to be difappointed and unhappy, I will conceal the anguifh I cannot diffipate; and the tightened cord of life or reafon will at laft fnap, and fet me free.

Yes; I fhall be happy—This heart is worthy of the blifs its feelings anticipate—and I cannot even perfuade myfelf, wretched as they have made me, that my principles and fentiments are not founded in nature and truth. But to have done with thefe fubjects.

— — — — — — —

— — — — — — —

— — — — — — —

I have been ferioufly employed in this way fince I came to ——; yet I never was fo much in the air.—I walk, I ride on horfeback—row, bathe, and even fleep sleep in the fields; my health is confequently improved. The child, ———— informs me, is well. I long to be with her.

Write to me immediately—were I only to think of myself, I could wish you to return to me, poor, with the simplicity of character, part of which you seem lately to have lost, that first attached to you.

Yours most affectionately

* * * *   * * * * *

I have been subscribing other letters —so I mechanically did the same to yours.

LETTER

L E T T E R LXI.

August 5.

EMPLOYMENT and exercife have been of great fervice to me ; and I have entirely recovered the ftrength and activity I loft during the time of my nurfing. I have feldom been in better health ; and my mind, though trembling to the touch of anguifh, is calmer —yet ftill the fame.—I have, it is true, enjoyed fome tranquillity, and more happinefs here, than for a long—long time paft.—(I fay happinefs, for I can give no other appellation to the exquifite delight this wild country and fine fummer have afforded me.)—Still, on examining my heart, I find that it is fo

constituted,

conftituted, I cannot live without fome
particular affection—I am afraid not
without a paffion—and I feel the want
of it more in fociety, than in folitude—

— — — — — —

— — — — — —

— — — — — —

Writing to you, whenever an affectionate epithet occurs—my eyes fill
with tears, and my trembling hand
ftops—you may then depend on my refolution, when with you.   If I am
doomed to be unhappy, I will confine
my anguifh in my own bofom—tendernefs, rather than paffion, has made me
fometimes overlook delicacy—the fame
tendernefs will in future reftrain me.
God blefs you!

LETTER

LETTER LXII.

August 7.

AIR, exercife, and bathing, have reftored me to health, braced my muf- cles, and covered my ribs, even whilft I have recovered my former activity.— I cannot tell you that my mind is calm, though I have fnatched fome moments of exquifite delight, wandering through the woods, and refting on the rocks.

This ftate of fufpenfe, my friend, is intolerable; we muft determine on fomething—and foon;—we muft meet fhortly, or part for ever. I am fen- fible that I acted foolifhly—but I was wretched—when we were together— Expecting too much, I let the pleafure
I might

I might have caught, flip from me. I cannot live with you—I ought not—if you form another attachment. But I promife you, mine fhall not be intruded on you. Little reafon have I to expect a fhadow of happinefs, after the cruel difappointments that have rent my heart; but that of my child feems to depend on our being together. Still I do not wifh you to facrifice a chance of enjoyment for an uncertain good. I feel a conviction, that I can provide for her, and it fhall be my object—if we are indeed to part to meet no more. Her affection muft not be divided. She muft be a comfort to me—if I am to have no other—and only know me as her fupport. - I feel that I cannot endure the anguifh of correfponding with you—if we are only to correfpond.—No; if you feek for happinefs

nefs elfewhere, my letters fhall not interrupt your repofe. I will be dead to
you. I cannot exprefs to you what
pain it gives me to write about an eternal feparation.—You muft determine—
examine yourfelf—But, for God's fake!
fpare me the anxiety of uncertainty!—
I may fink under the trial; but I will
not complain.

Adieu! If I had any thing more to
fay to you, it is all flown, and abforbed
by the moft tormenting apprehenfions;
yet I fcarcely know what new form of
mifery I have to dread.

I ought to beg your pardon for having fometimes written peevifhly; but
you will impute it to affection, if you
underftand any thing of the heart of

Yours truly

* * * *

LETTER

LETTER LXIII.

Auguft 9.

FIVE of your letters have been fent after me from ——. One, dated the 14th of July, was written in a ftyle which I may have merited, but did not expect from you. However this is not a time to reply to it, except to affure you that you fhall not be tormented with any more complaints. I am difgufted with myfelf for having fo long importuned you with my affection.——

My child is very well. We fhall foon meet, to part no more, I hope—I mean, I and my girl.—I fhall wait with fome degree

degree of anxiety till I am informed
how your affairs terminate.

Yours sincerely

* * * *

LETTER LXIV.

August 26.

I ARRIVED here last night, and with
the most exquisite delight, once more
pressed my babe to my heart. We
shall part no more. You perhaps cannot conceive the pleasure it gave me, to
see her run about, and play alone. Her
increasing intelligence attaches me more
and more to her. I have promised her that
I will fulfil my duty to her; and nothing
in

in future fhall make me forget it. I
will aifo exert myfelf to obtain an independence for her; but I will not be
too anxious on this head.

I have already told you, that I have
recovered my health. Vigour, and
even vivacity of mind, have returned
with a renovated conftitution. As for
peace, we will not talk of it. I was
not made, perhaps, to enjoy the calm
contentment fo termed.—

— — — — — —
— — — — — —
— — — — — —

You tell me that my letters tor-
ture you; I will not defcribe the ef-
feɛt yours have on me. l received
three this morning, the laft dated the
7th of this month. I mean not to give
vent to the emotions they produced.—
Certainly

are undisturbed. I had a dislike to living in England; but painful feelings
must give way to superior considera-
tions. I may not be able to acquire
the sum necessary to maintain my child
and self elsewhere. It is too late to go to
Switzerland. I shall not remain at ——,
living expensively. But be not alarmed!
I shall not force myself on you any
more.

Adieu! I am agitated—my whole
frame is convulsed—my lips tremble,
as if shook by cold, though fire seems to
be circulating in my veins.

God bless you.

* * * *

LETTER

LETTER LXV.

September 6.

I RECEIVED juft now your letter of the 20th. I had written you a letter laft night, into which imperceptibly flipt fome of my bitternefs of foul. I will copy the part relative to bufinefs. I am not fufficiently vain to imagine that I can, for more than a moment, cloud your enjoyment of life——to prevent even that, you had better never hear from me—and repofe on the idea that I am happy.

Gracious God! It is impoffible for me to ftifle fomething like refentment, when I receive frefh proofs of your in-difference.

difference. What I have fuffered this laft year, is not to be forgotten! I have not that happy fubftitute for wifdom, infenfibility—and the lively fympathies which bind me to my fellow-creatures, are all of a painful kind.—They are the agonies of a broken heart —pleafure and I have fhaken hands.

I fee here nothing but heaps of ruins, and only converfe with people immerfed in trade and fenfuality.

I am weary of travelling—yet feem to have no home—no refting place to look to.—I am ftrangely caft off.—How often, paffing through the rocks, I have thought, " But for this child, I would lay my head on one of them, and never open my eyes again!" With a heart feelingly alive to all the affections of my nature—I have never met with one, fofter than the ftone that I would fain

take

take for my laſt pillow. I once thought
I had, but it was all a deluſion. I meet
with families continually, who are
bound together by affection or principle—and, when I am conſcious that I
have fulfilled the duties of my ſtation,
almoſt to a forgetfulneſs of myſelf, I
am ready to demand, in a murmuring
tone, of Heaven, " Why am I thus
abandoned ?"

You ſay now   —   —   —

—   —   —   —   —   —

—   —   —   —   —   —

I do not underſtand you. It is necef-
ſary for you to write more explicitly—
and determine on ſome mode of conduct.—I cannot endure this ſuſpenſe—
Decide—Do you fear to ſtrike another
blow ? We live together, or eternally
part !—I ſhall not write to you again,
till I receive an anſwer to this. I muſt
compoſe

compofe my tortured foul, before I write on indifferent fubjeƈts. —   —

—   —   —   —   —   —

—   —   —   —   —   —

I do not know whether I write intelligibly, for my head is difturbed.—But this you ought to pardon—for it is with difficulty frequently that I make out what you mean to fay—You write, I fuppofe, at Mr. ——'s after dinner, when your head is not the cleareft—and as for your heart, if you have one, I fee nothing like the diƈtates of affeƈtion, unlefs a glimpfe when you mention the child.—Adieu!

LETTER

LETTER LXVI.

September 25.

I HAVE juft finifhed a letter, to be given in charge to captain ———. In that I complained of your filence, and expreffed my furprife that three mails fhould have arrived without bringing a line for me. Since I clofed it, I hear of another, and ftill no letter.—I am labouring to write calmly—this filence is a refinement on cruelty. Had captain ——— remained a few days longer, I would have returned with him to England. What have I to do here? I have repeatedly

written

written to you fully.　Do you do the same—and quickly.　Do not leave me in ſuſpenſe.　I have not deſerved this of you.　I cannot write, my mind is ſo diſtreſſed.　Adieu !

＊ ＊ ＊ ＊

END VOL. III.

POSTHUMOUS WORKS

OF

MARY WOLLSTONECRAFT GODWIN.

VOL. IV.

POSTHUMOUS WORKS

OF THE

AUTHOR

OF A

VINDICATION OF THE RIGHTS OF WOMAN.

IN FOUR VOLUMES.

VOL. IV.

LONDON:

PRINTED FOR J. JOHNSON, NO. 72, ST. PAUL'S
CHURCH-YARD; AND G. G. AND J. ROBINSON,
PATERNOSTER-ROW.
1798.

LETTERS

AND

MISCELLANEOUS PIECES.

IN TWO VOLUMES.

VOL. II.

LETTERS.

LETTER LXVII.

September 27.

WHEN you receive this, I shall either have landed, or be hovering on the British coast—your letter of the 18th decided me.

By what criterion of principle or affection, you term my questions extraordinary and unnecessary, I cannot determine.—You desire me to decide—I

had

had decided. You muſt have had long ago two letters of mine, from ———, to the ſame purport, to conſider.—In theſe, God knows! there was but too much affection, and the agonies of a diſtracted mind were but too faithfully pourtrayed!—What more then had I to ſay?—The negative was to come from you.—You had perpetually recurred to your promiſe of meeting me in the autumn—Was it extraordinary that I ſhould demand a yes, or no?—Your letter is written with extreme harſhneſs, coldneſs I am accuſtomed to, in it I find not a trace of the tenderneſs of humanity, much leſs of friendſhip.—I only ſee a deſire to heave a load off your ſhoulders.

I am above diſputing about words.—It matters not in what terms you decide.

The

The tremendous power who formed
this heart, muſt have foreſeen that, in
a world in which ſelf-intereſt, in various ſhapes, is the principal mobile, I
had little chance of eſcaping miſery.—
To the fiat of fate I ſubmit.—I am content to be wretched; but I will not be
contemptible.—Of me you have no
cauſe to complain, but for having had
too much regard for you—for having
expected a degree of permanent happineſs, when you only ſought for a
momentary gratification.

I am ſtrangely deficient in ſagacity.—
Uniting myſelf to you, your tenderneſs
ſeemed to make me amends for all my
former misfortunes.—On this tenderneſs and affection with what confidence
did I reſt!—but I leaned on a ſpear, that
has pierced me to the heart.——You
have thrown off a faithful friend, to
purſue

purſue the caprices of the moment.—
We certainly are differently organized;
for even now, when conviction has
been ſtamped on my ſoul by ſorrow, I
can ſcarcely believe it poſſible. It depends at preſent on you, whether you
will ſee me or not.—I ſhall take no
ſtep, till I ſee or hear from you.

Preparing myſelf for the worſt—I
have determined, if your next letter be
like the laſt, to write to Mr. ————
to procure me an obſcure lodging, and
not to inform any body of my arrival.—
There I will endeavour in a few months
to obtain the ſum neceſſary to take me
to France—from you I will not receive
any more.—I am not yet ſufficiently
humbled to depend on your beneficence.

Some people, whom my unhappi-
neſs has intereſted, though they know

not

not the extent of it, will affift me to
attain the object I have in view, the
independence of my child. Should a
peace take place, ready money will go
a great way in France—and I will borrow a fum, which my induftry *fhall*
enable me to pay at my leifure, to pur-
chafe a fmall eftate for my girl.—The
affiftance I fhall find neceffary to com-
plete her education, I can get at an
eafy rate at Paris—I can introduce her
to fuch fociety as fhe will like—and
thus, fecuring for her all the chance
for happinefs, which depends on me, I
fhall die in peace, perfuaded that the
felicity which has hitherto cheated
my expectation, will not always elude
my grafp. No poor tempeft-toffed
mariner ever more earneftly longed to
arrive at his port.

* * * *

I fhall

I ſhall not come up in the veſſel all the way, becauſe I have no place to go to. Captain ———— will inform you where I am. It is needleſs to add, that I am not in a ſtate of mind to bear ſuſpenſe—and that I wiſh to ſee you, though it be for the laſt time.

———————

LETTER LXVIII.

Sunday, October 4.

I WROTE to you by the packet, to inform you, that your letter of the 18th of laſt month, had determined me to ſet out with captain ————; but, as we ſailed very quick, I take it for granted, that you have not yet received it.

You

You say, I muſt decide for myſelf.—
I had decided, that it was moſt for the
intereſt of my little girl, and for my
own comfort, little as I expect, for us
to live together; and I even thought
that you would be glad, ſome years
hence, when the tumult of buſineſs was
over, to repoſe in the ſociety of an affectionate friend, and mark the progreſs
of our intereſting child, whilſt endeavouring to be of uſe in the circle you
at laſt reſolved to reſt in; for you cannot run about for ever..

From the tenour of your laſt letter
however, I am led to imagine, that you
have formed ſome new attachment.—
If it be ſo, let me earneſtly requeſt you
to ſee me once more, and immediately.
This is the only proof I require of the
friendſhip you profeſs for me. I will
then

then decide, fince you boggle about **a** mere form.

I am labouring to write with calm-nefs—but the extreme anguifh I feel, at landing without having any friend to receive me, and even to be con-fcious that the friend whom I moft wifh to fee, will feel a difagreeable fenfation at being informed of my arrival, does not come under the defcription of com-mon mifery. Every emotion yields to an overwhelming flood of forrow—and the playfulnefs of my child dif-treffes me.—On her account, I wifhed to remain a few days here, comfortlefs as is my fituation.—Befides, I did not wifh to furprife you. You have told me, that you would make any facrifice to promote my happinefs—and, even in your laft unkind letter, you talk of the ties which bind you to me and my child.

child.—Tell me, that you wish it, and I will cut this Gordian knot.

I now moft earneftly intreat you to write to me, without fail, by the return of the poft. Direct your letter to be left at the poft-office, and tell me whether you will come to me here, or where you will meet me. I can receive your letter on Wednefday morning.

Do not keep me in fufpenfe.—I expect nothing from you, or any human being: my die is caft!—I have fortitude enough to determine to do my duty; yet I cannot raife my depreffed fpirits, or calm my trembling heart.— That being who moulded it thus, knows that I am·unable to tear up by the roots the propenfity to affection which has been the torment of my life —but life will have an end !

Should

Should you come here (a few months
ago I could not have doubted it) you
will find me at ————. If you prefer
meeting me on the road, tell me where.

Yours affectionately

* * * *

————————————

L E T T E R LXIX.

I WRITE you now on my knees; im-
ploring you to send my child and the
maid with ——, to Paris, to be confign-
ed to the care of Madame ——, rue
——, fection de ——. Should they be
removed, —— can give their direction.

Let the maid have all my clothes,
without diftinction.

Pray

Pray pay the cook her wages, and do not mention the confeffion which I forced from her—a little fooner or later is of no confequence. Nothing but my extreme ftupidity could have rendered me blind fo long. Yet, whilft you affured me that you had no attachment, I thought we might ftill have lived together.

I fhall make no comments on your conduct; or any appeal to the world. Let my wrongs fleep with me! Soon, very foon fhall I be at peace. When you receive this, my burning head will be cold.

I would encounter a thoufand deaths, rather than a night like the laft. Your treatment has thrown my mind into a ftate of chaos; yet I am ferene. I go to find comfort, and my only fear is, that my poor body will be infulted by

an

an endeavour to recal my hated exiftence. But I fhall plunge into the
Thames where there is the leaft chance
of my being fnatched from the death I
feek.

God blefs you! May you never know
by experience what you have made me
endure. Should your fenfibility ever
awake, remorfe will find its way to your
heart ; and, in the midft of bufinefs and
fenfual pleafure, I fhall appear before
you, the victim of your deviation from
rectitude.   * * * *

LETTER

LETTER LXX.

Sunday Morning.

I HAVE only to lament, that, when the bitterneſs of death was paſt, I was inhumanly brought back to life and miſery. But a fixed determination is not to be baffled by diſappointment; nor will I allow that to be a frantic attempt, which was one of the calmeſt acts of reaſon. In this reſpect, I am only accountable to myſelf. Did I care for what is termed reputation, it is by other circumſtances that I ſhould be diſhonoured.

You ſay, " that you know not how to extricate ourſelves out of the wretchedneſs into which we have been plunged."

You

You are extricated long fince.—But I forbear to comment.——If I am condemned to live longer, it is a living death.

It appears to me, that you lay much more ftrefs on delicacy, than on principle; for I am unable to difcover what fentiment of delicacy would have been violated, by your vifiting a wretched friend—if indeed you have any friendfhip for me.—But fince your new attachment is the only thing facred in your eyes, I am filent—Be happy! My complaints fhall never more damp your enjoyment—perhaps I am miftaken in fuppofing that even my death could, for more than a moment.—This is what you call magnanimity —It is happy for yourfelf, that you poffefs this quality in the higheft degree.

Your continually afferting, that you will

will do all in your power to contribute to my comfort (when you only allude to pecuniary affiftance), appears to me a flagrant breach of delicacy.—I want not fuch vulgar comfort, nor will I accept it. I never wanted but your heart—That gone, you have nothing more to give. Had I only poverty to fear, I fhould not fhrink from life.— Forgive me then, if I fay, that I fhall confider any direct or indirect attempt to fupply my neceffities, as an infult which I have not merited—and as rather done out of tendernefs for your own reputation, than for me. Do not miftake me; I do not think that you value money (therefore I will not accept what you do not care for) though I do much lefs, becaufe certain privations are not painful to me.

When

When I am dead, refpect for yourfelf
will make you take care of the child.

I write with difficulty—probably I
fhall never write to you again.—Adieu!

God blefs you!

                       ✳ ✳ ✳ ✳

LETTER LXXI.

Monday Morning,

I am compelled at laft to fay that
you treat me ungeneroufly. I agree
with you, that   —   —   —

—   —   —   —   —   —

—   —   —   —   —   —

—   —   —   —   —   —

—   —   —   —   —   —

                            But

But let the obliquity now fall on me.—
I fear neither poverty nor infamy. I am
unequal to the tafk of writing—and
explanations are not neceffary. —

— — — — — — —

— — — — — — —

My child may have to blufh for her
mother's want of prudence—and may
lament that the rectitude of my heart
made me above vulgar precautions;
but fhe fhall not defpife me for mean-
nefs.—You are now perfectly free.—
God blefs you.

* * * *

LETTER

LETTER LXXIII.

Saturday Night,

I HAVE been hurt by indirect enquiries, which appear to me not to be
dictated by any tendernefs to me.—You
afk " If I am well or tranquil?"—They
who think me fo, muft want a heart to
eftimate my feelings by.—I chufe
then to be the organ of my own fentiments.

I muft tell you, that I am very much
mortified by your continually offering
me pecuniary affiftance—and, confidering your going to the new houfe, as an
open avowal that you abandon me, let
me

me tell you that I will fooner perifh than receive any thing from you—and I fay this at the moment when I am difappointed in my firft attempt to obtain a temporary fupply. But this even pleafes me; an accumulation of difappointments and misfortunes feems to fuit the habit of my mind.—

Have but a little patience, and I will remove myfelf where it will not be neceffary for you to talk—of courfe, not to think of me. But let me fee, written by yourfelf—for I will not receive it through any other medium—that the affair is finifhed.—It is an infult to me to fuppofe, that I can be reconciled, or recover my fpirits; but, if you hear nothing of me, it will be the fame thing to you.

 * * * *

Even

Even your feeing me, has been to oblige other people, and not to footh my diftracted mind.

———————

L E T T E R LXXIV.

Thurfday Afternoon.

Mr. ——— having forgot to defire you to fend the things of mine which were left at the houfe, I have to requeft you to let ——— bring them o ————.

I fhall go this evening to the lodging; fo you need not be reftrained from coming here to tranfact your bufinefs.— And, whatever I may think, and feel—

you

you need not fear that I fhall publicly complain—No ! If I have any criterion to judge of right and wrong, I have been moft ungeneroufly treated : but, wifhing now only to hide myfelf, I fhall be filent as the grave in which I long to forget myfelf. I fhall protect and provide for my child.—I only mean by this to fay, that you having nothing to fear from my defperation.

Farewel.

✿ ✳ ✿ ✦

LETTER

LETTER LXXV.

London, November 27.

THE letter, without an addrefs, which you put up with the letters you returned, did not meet my eyes till juft now.—I had thrown the letters afide—I did not wifh to look over a regifter of forrow.

My not having feen it, will account for my having written to you with anger—under the impreffion your departure, without even a line left for me, made on me, even after your late conduct, which could not lead me to expect much attention to my fufferings.

In fact, " the decided conduct, which
                    appeared

appeared to me fo unfeeling," has almoft overturned my reafon ; my mind
is injured—I fcarcely know where I
am, or what I do.—The grief I cannot
conquer (for fome cruel recollections
never quit me, banifhing almoft every
other) I labour to conceal in total
folitude.—My life therefore is but an
exercife of fortitude, continually on
the ftretch—and hope never gleams in
this tomb, where I am buried alive.

But I meant to reafon with you, and
not to complain.—You tell me, " that I
fhall judge more coolly of your mode
of acting, fome time hence." But is it
not poffible that *paffion* clouds your reafon, as much as it does mine?—and
ought you not to doubt, whether thofe
principles are fo " exalted," as you
term them, which only lead to your
own gratification? In other words,
whether

whether it be juft to have no principle of action, but that of following your inclination, trampling on the affection you have foftered, and the expectations you have excited?

My affection for you is rooted in my heart.—I know you are not what you now feem—nor will you always act, or feel, as you now do, though I may never be comforted by the change.—Even at Paris, my image will haunt you.—You will fee my pale face—and fometimes the tears of anguifh will drop on your heart, which you have forced from mine.

I cannot write. I thought I could quickly have refuted all your *ingenious* arguments ; but my head is confufed.—Right or wrong, I am miferable!

It feems to me, that my conduct has always been governed by the ftricteft principles of juftice and truth.—Yet, how

how wretched have my focial feelings, and delicacy of fentiment rendered me! —I have loved with my whole foul, only to difcover that I had no chance of a return—and that exiftence is a burthen without it.

I do not perfectly underftand you.— If, by the offer of your friendfhip, you ftill only mean pecuniary fupport—I muft again reject it.—Trifling are the ills of poverty in the fcale of my misfortunes.—God blefs you!

* * * *

I have been treated ungeneroufly— if I underftand what is generofity.—— You feem to me only to have been anxious to fhake me off—regardlefs whether you dafhed me to atoms by the fall.— In truth I have been rudely handled. *Do you judge coolly,* and I truft
you

you will not continue to call thofe ca-
pricious feelings " the moft refined,"
which would undermine not only the
moft facred principles, but the affections which unite mankind.——You
would render mothers unnatural—and
there would be no fuch thing as a father!—If your theory of morals is the
moft " exalted," it is certainly the moft
eafy.—It does not require much magnanimity, to determine to pleafe ourfelves for the moment, let others fuffer what they will!

Excufe me for again tormenting you,
my heart thirfts for juftice from you—
and whilft I recollect that you approved
Mifs ———'s conduct—I am convinced you will not always juftify your
own.

Beware of the deceptions of paffion!
It will not always banifh from your
mind,

mind, that you have acted ignobly—and condefcended to fubterfuge to glofs over the conduct you could not excufe.—Do truth and principle require fuch facrifices?

———————

LETTER LXXVI.

London, December 8.

HAVING juft been informed that —— is to return immediately to Paris, I would not mifs a fure opportunity of writing, becaufe I am not certain that my laft, by Dover has reached you.

Refentment, and even anger, are momentary emotions with me—and
I wifhed

I wifhed to tell you fo, that if you ever
think of me, it may not be in the light
of an enemy.

That I have not been ufed *well* I
muft ever feel; perhaps, not always
with the keen anguifh I do at prefent—
for I began even now to write calmly,
and I cannot reftrain my tears.

I am ftunned!—Your late conduct
ftill appears to me a frightful dream.—
Ah! afk yourfelf if you have not condefcended to employ a little addrefs, I
could almoft fay cunning, unworthy of
you?—Principles are facred things—
and we never play with truth, with
impunity.

The expectation (I have too fondly
nourifhed it) of regaining your affection, every day grows fainter and
fainter.—Indeed, it feems to me, when
I am more fad than ufual, that I fhall
never

never fee you more.—Yet you will not
always forget me.—You will feel fomething like remorfe, for having lived only
for yourfelf—and facrificed my peace
to inferior gratifications. In a comfortlefs old age, you will remember
that you had one difinterefted friend,
whofe heart you wounded to the quick.
The hour of recollection will come—
and you will not be fatisfied to act the
part of a boy, till you fall into that of a
dotard. I know that your mind, your
heart, and your principles of action,
are all fuperior to your prefent conduct.
You do, you muft, refpect me—and
you will be forry to forfeit my efteem.

You know beft whether I am ftill
preferving the remembrance of an
imaginary being.—I once thought that
I knew you thoroughly—but now I
am obliged to leave fome doubts that
                              involuntarily

Certainly you are right; our minds are not congenial. I have lived in an ideal world, and foftered fentiments that you do not comprehend—or you would not treat me thus. I am not, I will not be, merely an object of compaffion—a clog, however light, to teize you. Forget that I exift: I will never remind you. Something emphatical whifpers me to put an end to thefe ftruggles. Be free—I will not torment, when I cannot pleafe. I can take care of my child; you need not continually tell me that our fortune is infeparable, *that you will try to cherifh tendernefs* for me. Do no violence to yourfelf! When we are feparated, our intereft, fince you give fo much weight to pecuniary confiderations, will be entirely divided. I want not protection without affection; and fupport I need not, whilft my faculties are involuntarily prefs on me, to be cleared up by time.

You may render me unhappy; but cannot make me contemptible in my own eyes.—I fhall ftill be able to fupport my child, though I am difappointed in fome other plans of ufefulnefs, which I once believed would have afforded you equal pleafure.

Whilft I was with you, I reftrained my natural generofity, becaufe I thought your property in jeopardy.—When I went to —————, I requefted you, *if you could conveniently*, not to forget my father, fifters, and fome other people, whom I was interefted about.—Money was lavifhed away, yet not only my requefts were neglected, but fome trifling debts were not difcharged, that now come on me.—Was this friendfhip—or generofity ? Will you not grant

you

you have forgotten yourfelf? Still
I have an affection for you.—God
blefs you.

* * * *

LETTER LXXVII.

As the parting from you for ever is
the moft ferious event of my life, I will
once expoftulate with you, and call
not the language of truth and feeling
ingenuity!

I know the foundnefs of your underftanding—and know that it is impoffible for you always to confound the
caprices of every wayward inclination
with the manly dictates of principle.

You

You tell me " that I torment you."—
Why do I?——Becaufe you cannot
eftrange your heart entirely from me—
and you feel that juftice is on my fide.
You urge, " that your conduct was
unequivocal."-—It was not.—-When
your coolnefs has hurt me, with what
tendernefs have you endeavoured to
remove the impreffion!—and even before I returned to England, you took
great pains to convince me, that all
my uneafinefs was occafioned by the
effect of a worn-out conftitution—and
you concluded your letter with thefe
words, " Bufinefs alone has kept me
from you.—Come to any port, and I
will fly down to my two dear girls
with a heart all their own."

With thefe affurances, is it extraordinary that I fhould believe what I
wifhed? I might—and did think that
you

you had a ſtruggle with old propenſi-
ties; but I ſtill thought that I and virtue ſhould at laſt prevail. I ſtill thought
that you had a magnanimity of cha-
raĉter, which would enable you to conquer yourſelf.

————, believe me, it is not
romance, you have acknowledged to
me feelings of this kind.—You could
reſtore me to life and hope, and the
ſatisfaĉtion you would feel, would
amply repay you.

In tearing myſelf from you, it is my
own heart I pierce—and the time will
come, when you will lament that you
have thrown away a heart, that, even
in the moment of paſſion, you cannot
deſpiſe.—I would owe every thing to
your generoſity—but, for God's ſake,
keep me no longer in ſuſpenſe!—Let
me ſee you once more!—

LETTER

LETTER LXXVIII.

You muſt do as you pleaſe with reſpect to the child.—I could wiſh that it might be done ſoon, that my name may be no more mentioned to you. It is now finiſhed.—Convinced that you have neither regard nor friendſhip, I diſdain to utter a reproach, though I have had reaſon to think, that the " forbearance" talked of, has not been very delicate.—It is however of no conſequence.—I am glad you are ſatiſ-fied with your own conduct.

I now ſolemnly aſſure you, that this is an eternal farewel.—Yet I flinch not from the duties which tie me to life.

That

That there is " fophiftry" on one
fide or other, is certain; but now it
matters not on which. On my part it
has not been a queftion of words. Yet
your underftanding or mine muft be
ftrangely warped—for what you term
" delicacy," appears to me to be exactly the contrary. I have no criterion
for morality, and have thought in vain,
if the fenfations which lead you to follow an ancle or ftep, be the facred
foundation of principle and affection.
Mine has been of a very different nature, or it would not have ftood the
brunt of your farcafms.

The fentiment in me is ftill facred.
If there be any part of me that will
furvive the fenfe of my misfortunes, it
is the purity of my affections. The
impetuofity of your fenfes, may have
led you to term mere animal defire, the
fource

fource of principle ; and it may give zeſt to fome years to come.—Whether you will always think fo, I ſhall never know.

It is ſtrange that, in fpite of all you do, fomething like conviction forces me to believe, that you are not what you appear to be.

I part with you in peace.

LETTER

LETTER

ON THE

PRESENT CHARACTER

OF THE

FRENCH NATION.

LETTER

*Introductory to a Series of Letters on the Pre-
sent Character of the French Nation.*

———————

Paris, February 15, 1793.

My dear friend,

IT is neceſſary perhaps for an obſerver
of mankind, to guard as carefully the
remembrance of the firſt impreſſion
made by a nation, as by a countenance ;
becauſe we imperceptibly loſe ſight of
the national character, when we become more intimate with individuals.
It is not then uſeleſs or preſumptuous
to note, that, when I firſt entered Paris,
the

the striking contrast of riches and poverty, elegance and slovenliness, urba-
nity and deceit, every where caught
my eye, and saddened my soul; and
these impressions are still the foundation
of my remarks on the manners, which
flatter the senses, more than they interest the heart, and yet excite more interest than esteem.

The whole mode of life here tends
indeed to render the people frivolous,
and, to borrow their favourite epithet,
amiable.   Ever on the wing, they are
always sipping the sparkling joy on the
brim of the cup, leaving satiety in the
bottom for those who venture to drink
deep.   On all sides they trip along,
buoyed up by animal spirits, and seem-
ingly so void of care, that often, when
I am walking on the *Boulevards*, it
occurs to me, that they alone understand
the

the full import of the term leifure; and they trifle their time away with fuch an air of contentment, I know not how to wifh them wifer at the expence of their gaiety. They play before me like motes in a funbeam, enjoying the pafling ray; whilft an Englifh head, fearching for more folid happinefs, lofes, in the analyfis of pleafure, the volatile fweets of the moment. Their chief enjoyment, it is true, rifes from vanity: but it is not the vanity that engenders vexation of fpirit; on the contrary, it lightens the heavy burthen of life, which reafon too often weighs, merely to fhift from one fhoulder to the other.

Inveftigating the modification of the paffion, as I would analyze the elements that give a form to dead matter, I fhall attempt to trace to their fource the

the caufes which have combined to
render this nation the moft polifhed, in
a phyfical fenfe, and probably the moft
fuperficial in the world; and I mean to
follow the windings of the various
ftreams that difembogue into a terrific
gulf, in which all the dignity of our
nature is abforbed. For every thing
has confpired to make the French the
moft fenfual people in the world; and
what can render the heart fo hard, or
fo effectually ftifle every moral emotion,
as the refinements of fenfuality?

The frequent repetition of the word
French, appears invidious; let me then
make a previous obfervation, which I
beg you not to lofe fight of, when I
fpeak rather harfhly of a land flowing
with milk and honey. Remember that
it is not the morals of a particular
people that I would decry; for are we
not

not all of the fame ftock? But I wifh calmly to confider the ftage of civilization in which I find the French, and, giving a fketch of their character, and unfolding the circumftances which have produced its identity, I fhall endeavour to throw fome light on the hiftory of man, and on the prefent important fubjects of difcuffion.

I would I could firft inform you that, out of the chaos of vices and follies, prejudices and virtues, rudely jumbled together, I faw the fair form of Liberty flowly rifing, and Virtue expanding her wings to fhelter all her children! I fhould then hear the account of the barbarities that have rent the bofom of France patiently, and blefs the firm hand that lopt off the rotten limbs. But, if the ariftocracy of birth is levelled with the ground, only to make room

for

for that of riches, I am afraid that the morals of the people will not be much improved by the change, or the government rendered lefs venal. Still it is not juft to dwell on the mifery produced by the prefent ftruggle, without adverting to the ftanding evils of the old fyftem. I am grieved—forely grieved —when I think of the blood that has ftained the caufe of freedom at Paris; but I alfo hear the fame live ftream cry aloud from the highways, through which the retreating armies paffed with famine and death in their rear, and I hide my face with awe before the infcrutable ways of providence, fweeping in fuch various directions the befom of deftruction over the fons of men.

Before I came to France, I cherifhed, you know, an opinion, that ftrong virtues

tues might exift with the polifhed manners produced by the progrefs of civilization; and I even anticipated the
epoch, when, in the courfe of improvement, men would labour to become
virtuous, without being goaded on by
mifery. But now, the perfpective of
the golden age, fading before the attentive eye of obfervation, almoft eludes
my fight; and, lofing thus in part my
theory of a more perfect ftate, ftart not,
my friend, if I bring forward an opinion, which at the firft glance feems to
be levelled againft the exiftence of God!
I am not become an Atheift, I affure
you, by refiding at Paris: yet I begin
to fear that vice, or, if you will, evil,
is the grand mobile of action, and that,
when the paffions are juftly poized, we
become harmlefs, and in the fame proportion ufelefs.

The

The wants of reafon are very few; and, were we to confider difpaffionately the real value of moft things, we fhould probably reft fatisfied with the fimple gratification of our phyfical neceffities, and be content with negative goodnefs: for it is frequently, only that wanton, the Imagination, with her artful coquetry, who lures us forward, and makes us run over a rough road, pufhing afide every obftacle merely to catch a difappointment.

The defire alfo of being ufeful to others, is continually damped by experience; and, if the exertions of humanity were not in fome meafure their own reward, who would endure mifery, or ftruggle with care, to make fome people ungrateful, and others idle?

You will call thefe melancholy effufions,

fions, and guefs that, fatigued by the vivacity, which has all the buftling folly of childhood, without the inno- cence which renders ignorance charm- ing, I am too fevere in my ftrictures. It may be fo ; and I am aware that the good effects of the revolution will be laft felt at Paris ; where furely the foul of Epicurus has long been at work to root out the fimple emotions of the heart, which, being natural, are always moral. Rendered cold and artificial by the felfifh enjoyments of the fenfes, which the government foftered, is it furprifing that fimplicity of manners, and finglenefs of heart, rarely appear, to recreate me with the wild odour of nature, fo paffing fweet?

Seeing how deep the fibres of mif- chief have fhot, I fometimes afk, with a doubting accent, Whether a nation can

go

go back to the purity of manners which
has hitherto been maintained unfullied
only by the keen air of poverty, when,
emafculated by pleafure, the luxuries
of profperity are become the wants of
nature? I cannot yet give up the hope,
that a fairer day is dawning on Europe,
though I muft hefitatingly obferve, that
little is to be expected from the narrow
principle of commerce which feems
every where to be fhoving afide *the point
of honour* of the *nobleffe*. I can look beyond the evils of the moment, and do
not expect muddied water to become
clear before it has had time to ftand;
yet, even for the moment, it is the
moft terrific of all fights, to fee men
vicious without warmth—to fee the
order that fhould be the fuperfcription
of virtue, cultivated to give fecurity to
crimes which only thoughtleffnefs could
palliate.

palliate. Diforder is, in fact, the very
effence of vice, though with the wild
wifhes of a corrupt fancy humane emotions often kindly mix to foften their
atrocity. Thus humanity, generofity,
and even felf-denial, fometimes render
a character grand, and even ufeful,
when hurried away by lawlefs paffions;
but what can equal the turpitude of a
cold calculator who lives for himfelf
alone, and confidering his fellow-creatures merely as machines of pleafure,
never forgets that honefty is the beft po-
licy? Keeping ever within the pale of
the law, he crufhes his thoufands with
impunity; but it is with that degree of
management, which makes him, to borrow a fignificant vulgarifm, a villain
in grain. The very excefs of his depra-
vation preferves him, whilft the more
refpectable beaft of prey, who prowls
about

about like the lion, and roars to an-
nounce his approach, falls into a fnare.

You may think it too foon to form
an opinion of the future government,
yet it is impoffible to avoid hazarding
fome conjectures, when every thing
whifpers me, that names, not principles, are changed, and when I fee that
the turn of the tide has left the dregs of
the old fyftem to corrupt the new. For
the fame pride of office, the fame defire
of power are ftill vifible; with this ag-
gravation, that, fearing to return to obfcurity after having but juft acquired
a relifh for diftinction, each hero, or
philofopher, for all are dubbed with
thefe new titles, endeavours to make
hay while the fun fhines; and every
petty municipal officer, become the idol,
or rather the tyrant of the day, ftalks
like a cock on a dunghil.

I fhall

I shall now conclude this desultory letter; which however will enable you to foresee that I shall treat more of morals than manners.

Yours ————·

FRAGMENT

OF

LETTERS

ON THE

MANAGEMENT OF INFANTS.

CONTENTS.

LETTERS

ON THE

MANAGEMENT OF INFANTS.

LETTER I.

I OUGHT to apologize for not having written to you on the subject you mentioned ; but, to tell you the truth, it grew upon me : and, instead of an answer, I have begun a series of letters on the management of children in their infancy. Replying then to your question, I have the public in my

thoughts,

thoughts, and fhall endeavour to fhow what modes appear to me neceffary, to render the infancy of children more healthy and happy. I have long thought, that the caufe which renders children as hard to rear as the moft fragile plant, is our deviation from fimplicity. I know that fome able phyficians have recommended the method I have purfued, and I mean to point out the good effects I have obferved in practice. I am aware that many matrons will exclaim againft me, and dwell on the number of children they have brought up, as their mothers did before them, without troubling themfelves with new-fangled notions; yet, though, in my uncle Toby's words, they fhould attempt to filence me, by " wifhing I had feen their large" families, I muft fuppofe, while a third part

of

of the human fpecies, according to the
moft accurate calculation, die during
their infancy, juft at the threfhold of
life, that there is fome error in the
modes adopted by mothers and nurfes,
which counteracts their own endeavours. I may be miftaken in fome
particulars ; for general rules, founded
on the foundeft reafon, demand individual modification ; but, if I can perfuade any of the rifing generation to
exercife their reafon on this head, I am
content. My advice will probably
be found moft ufeful to mothers in the
middle clafs ; and it is from them that
the lower imperceptibly gains improvement. Cuftom, produced by reafon in one, may fafely be the effect of
imitation in the other.— — —

LETTERS

TO

Mr. JOHNSON,

BOOKSELLER,

IN

St. PAUL's CHURCH-YARD.

LETTERS

TO

Mr. JOHNSON.

LETTER I.

Dublin, April 14, [1787.]

Dear ſir,

I AM ſtill an invalid—and begin to believe that I ought never to expect to enjoy health. My mind preys on my body—and, when I endeavour to be uſeful, I grow too much intereſted for my own peace. Confined almoſt entirely to the ſociety of children, I am anxiouſly ſolicitous for their future welfare, and mortified beyond meaſure,

when

when counteracted in my endeavours to improve them.—I feel all a mother's fears for the fwarm of little ones which furround me, and obferve diforders, without having power to apply the proper remedies. How can I be reconciled to life, when it is always a painful warfare, and when I am deprived of all the pleafures I relifh?—I allude to rational converfations, and domeftic affections. Here, alone, a poor folitary individual in a ftrange land, tied to one fpot, and fubject to the caprice of another, can I be contented? I am defirous to convince you that I have *fome* caufe for forrow—and am not without reafon detached from life. I fhall hope to hear that you are well, and am yours fincerely

MARY WOLLSTONECRAFT.

LETTER

LETTER II.

Henley, Thurfday, Sept. 23.

My dear fir,

Since I faw you, I have, literally
fpeaking, *enjoyed* folitude. My fifter
could not accompany me in my rambles; I therefore wandered alone, by
the fide of the Thames, and in the
neighbouring beautiful fields and
pleafure grounds : the profpects were
of fuch a placid kind, I *caught* tranquil
lity while I furveyed them—my mind
was *fill*, though active. Were I to
give you an account how I have fpent
my time, you would fmile.—I found an
old French bible here, and amufed
myfelf with comparing it with our
English

Englifh tranflation; then I would liften
to the falling leaves, or obferve the
various tints the autumn gave to
them—At other times, the finging of
a robin, or the noife of a water-mill,
engaged my attention—partial attention—, for I was, at the fame time
perhaps difcuffing fome knotty point,
or ftraying from this *tiny* world to new
fyftems.   After thefe excurfions, I returned to the family meals, told the
children ftories (they think me *vaftly*
agreeable), and my fifter was amufed.—
Well, will you allow me to call this
way of paffing my days pleafant?

I was juft going to mend my pen;
but I believe it will enable me to fay
all I have to add to this epiftle.   Have
you yet heard of an habitation for me?
I often think of my new plan of life;
and, left my fifter fhould try to prevail

on

on me to alter it, I have avoided mentioning it to her. I am determined!—Your fex generally laugh at female determinations; but let me tell you, I never yet refolved to do, any thing of confequence, that I did not adhere refolutely to it, till I had accomplifhed my purpofe, improbable as it might have appeared to a more timid mind. In the courfe of near nine-and-twenty years, I have gathered fome experience, and felt many *fevere* difappointments— and what is the amount? I long for a little peace and *independence!* Every obligation we receive from our fellow-creatures is a new fhackle, takes from our native freedom, and debafes the mind, makes us mere earthworms—I am not fond of grovelling!

I am, fir, yours, &c.

MARY WOLLSTONECRAFT.

LETTER

LETTER III.

Market Harborough, Sept. 20.

My dear fir,

You left me with three opulent tradefmen; their converfation was not calculated to beguile the way, when the fable curtain concealed the beauties of nature. I liftened to the tricks of trade—and fhrunk away, without wifhing to grow rich; even the novelty of the fubjects did not render them pleafing; fond as I am of tracing the paffions in all their different forms—I was not furprifed by any glimpfe of the fublime, or beautiful—though one of them imagined I fhould be a ufeful partner in a good *firm*. I was very much fatigued, and have fcarcely recovered myfelf.

myſelf. I do not expect to enjoy the ſame tranquil pleaſures Henley afford-ed : I meet with new objects to employ my mind ; but many painful emotions. are complicated with the reflections they give riſe to:

I do not intend to enter on the *old* topic, yet hope to hear from you—and am yours, &c.

MARY WOLLSTONECRAFT.

LETTER IV.

Friday Nighti

My dear ſir,

THOUGH your remarks are generally judicious—I cannot *now* concur with you, I mean with reſpect to the preface*,

* To Original Stories.

and

and have not altered it. I hate the
ufual fmooth way of exhibiting proud
humility. A general rule *only* extends
to the majority—and, believe me, the
few judicious parents who may perufe
my book, will not feel themfelves hurt—
and the weak are too vain to mind what
is faid in a book intended for children.

I return you the Italian MS.—but
do not haftily imagine that I am indolent. I would not fpare any labour to
do my duty—and, after the moft laborious day, that fingle thought would
folace me more than any pleafures the
fenfes could enjoy. I find I could not
tranflate the MS. well. If it was not
a MS, I fhould not be fo eafily intimi-
dated; but the hand, and errors in
orthography, or abbreviations, are a
ftumbling-block at the firft fetting
out.—I cannot bear to do any thing I
cannot

eannot do well—and I fhould lofe time in the vain attempt.

I had, the other day, the fatisfaction of again receiving a letter from my poor, dear Margaret*.—With all a mother's fondnefs I could tranfcribe a part of it—She fays, every day her affection to me, and dependence on heaven increafe, &c.——I mifs her innocent careffes—and fometimes indulge a pleafing hope, that fhe may be allowed to cheer my childlefs age—if I am to live to be old.—At any rate, I may hear of the virtues I may not contemplate—and my reafon may permit me to love a female.—I now allude to ————. I have received another letter from her, and her childifh complaints vex me—indeed they do—As ufual, good-night.   MARY.

* Countefs Mount Cafhel.

If

If parents attended to their children, I would not have written the ſtories; for, what are books—compared to converſations which affection inforces !—

———————

LETTER V.

My dear ſir,

REMEMBER you are to ſettle *my account*, as I want to know how much I am in your debt—but do not ſuppoſe that I feel any uneaſineſs on that ſcore. The generality of people in trade would not be much obliged to me for a like civility, *but you were a man* before you were a bookſeller—ſo I am your ſincere friend,

MARY.

LETTER

LETTER VI.

Friday Morning.

I AM fick with vexation—and wifh I could knock my foolifh head againft the wall, that bodily pain might make me feel lefs anguifh from felf-reproach! To fay the truth, I was never more difpleafed with myfelf, and I will tell you the caufe.—You may reeollect that I did not mention to you the circumftance of ———— having a fortune left to him; nor did a hint of it drop from me when I converfed with my fifter; becaufe I knew he had a fufficient motive for concealing it. Laft Sunday, when his character was afperfed, as I thought, unjuftly, in the heat of vindication

cation I informed ****** that he was now independent; but, at the same time, defired him not to repeat my information to B——; yet, laft Tuefday, he told him all—and the boy at B——'s gave Mrs. ——— an account of it. As Mr. ——— knew he had only made a confident of me (I blufh to think of it!) he guefled the channel of intelligence, and this morning came (not to reproach me, I wifh he had!) but to point out the injury I have done him.—Let what will be the confequence, I will reimburfe him, if I deny myfelf the neceffaries of life—and even then my folly will fting me.—Perhaps you can fcarcely conceive the mifery I at this moment endure—that I, whofe power of doing good is fo limited, fhould do harm, galls my very foul. ****** may laugh at thefe qualms—but, fuppofing Mr.

———— to be unworthy, I am not the lefs to blame. Surely it is hell to defpife one's felf!—I did not want this additional vexation—at this time I have many that hang heavily on my fpirits. I fhall not call on you this month—nor ftir out.—My ftomach has been fo fuddenly and violently affeĉted, I am unable to lean over the defk.

MARY WOLLSTONECRAFT.

LETTER VII.

As I am become a reviewer, I think it right, in the way of bufinefs, to confider the fubjeĉt. You have alarmed the editor of the Critical, as the advertifement prefixed to the Appendix plainly

plainly ſhows. The Critical appears
to me to be a timid, mean produ&ion,
and its ſuccefs is a reflection on the
taſte and judgment of the public ; but,
as a body, who ever gave it credit for
much ? The voice of the people is only
the voice of truth, when ſome man of
abilities has had time to get faſt hold of
the GREAT NOSE of the monſter. Of
courſe, local fame is generally a
clamour, and dies away. The Appendix to the Monthly afforded me more
amuſement, though every article almoſt
wants energy and a *cant* of virtue and
liberality is ſtrewed over it ; always
tame, and eager to pay court to eſta-
bliſhed fame. The account of Necker
is one unvaried tone of admiration.
Surely men were born only to provide
for the ſuſtenance of the body by en-
feebling the mind !   MARY.

LETTER

LETTER VIII.

You made me very low-fpirited laft night, by your manner of talking.—You are my only friend—the only perfon I am *intimate* with.—I never had a father, or a brother—you have been both to me, ever fince I knew you—yet I have fometimes been very petulant.—I have been thinking of thofe inftances of ill-humour and quicknefs, and they appeared like crimes.

Yours fincerely

MARY.

LETTER

LETTER IX.

Saturday Night.

I am a mere animal, and inftinctive emotions too often filence the fuggeftions of reafon. Your note—I can fcarcely tell why, hurt me—and produced a kind of winterly fmile, which diffufes a beam of defpondent tranquillity over the features. I have been very ill—Heaven knows it was more than fancy—After fome fleeplefs, wearifome nights, towards the morning I have grown delirious.—Laft Thurfday, in particular, I imagined ———— was thrown into great diftrefs by his folly; and I, unable to affift him, was in an agony. My nerves were in fuch a painful

painful ſtate of irritation—I ſuffered more than I can exprefs—Society was neceſſary—and might have diverted me till I gained more ſtrength; but I bluſhed when I recollected how often I had teazed you with childiſh complaints, and the reveries of a difordered imagination. I even *imagined* that I intruded on you, becaufe you never called on me—though you perceived that I was not well.—I have nouriſhed a fickly kind of delicacy, which gives me many unneceſſary pangs.—I acknowledge that life is but a jeſt—and often a frightful dream—yet catch myfelf every day fearching for fomething ferious—and feel real mifery from the difappointment. I am a ftrange compound of weaknefs and refolution! However, if I muſt fuffer, I will endeavour to fuffer in filence.

There

There is certainly a great defect in my mind—my wayward heart creates its own mifery—Why I am made thus I cannot tell; and, till I can form fome idea of the whole of my exiftence, I muft be content to weep and dance like a child—long for a toy, and be tired of it as foon as I get it.

We muft each of us wear a fool's cap; but mine, alas! has loft its bells, and is grown fo heavy, I find it intolerably troublefome.——Good-night! I have been purfuing a number of ftrange thoughts fince I began to write, and have actually both wept and laughed immoderately—Surely I am a fool—

MARY W.

LETTER

LETTER X.

Monday Mornihg.

I REALLY want a German grammar, as I intend to attempt to learn that language—and I will tell you the reafon why.—While I live, I am perfuaded, I muft exert my underftanding to pro-cure an independence, and render myfelf ufeful. To make the tafk eafier, I ought to ftore my mind with know-ledge—The feed time is paffing away. I fee the neceffity of labouring now—and of that neceffity I do not complain; on the contrary, l am thankful that I have more than common incentives to purfue knowledge, and draw my plea-

fures

fures from the employments that are within my reach. You perceive this is not a gloomy day—I feel at this moment particularly grateful to you—without your humane and *delicate* affiftance, how many obftacles fhould I not have had to encounter—too often fhould I have been out of patience with my fellow-creatures, whom I wifh to love !—Allow me to love you, my dear fir, and call friend a being I refpect.—Adieu !

MARY W.

LETTER

LETTER XI.

I THOUGHT you *very* unkind, nay, very unfeeling, laſt night. My cares and vexations—I will ſay what I allow myſelf to think—do me honour, as they ariſe from my diſintereſtedneſs and *unbending* principles; nor can that mode of conduct be a reflection on my underſtanding, which enables me to bear miſery, rather than ſelfiſhly live for myſelf alone. I am not the only character deſerving of relpect, that has had to ſtruggle with various ſorrows—while inferior minds have enjoyed local fame and preſent comfort.—Dr. Johnſon's cares almoſt drove him mad—but, I ſuppoſe, you would quietly have told him, he was a fool for not being calm, and that wiſe men ſtriving againſt the

ſtream,

ſtream, can yet be in good humour. I have done with infenſible human wiſdom,—" indifference cold in wiſdom's guiſe,"—and turn to the ſource of perfection—who perhaps never diſregarded an almoſt broken heart, eſpecially when a reſpect, a practical reſpect, for virtue, ſharpened the wounds of adverſity. I am ill—I ſtayed in bed this morning till eleven o'clock, only thinking of getting money to extricate myſelf out of ſome of my difficulties—The ſtruggle is now over. I will condeſcend to try to obtain ſome in a diſagreeable way.

Mr. —— called on me juſt now—pray did you know his motive for calling* ?—I think him impertinently offi-

* This alludes to a fooliſh propoſal of marriage for mercenary conſiderations, which the gentleman here mentioned thought proper to recommend to her. The two letters which immediately follow, are addreſſed to the gentleman himſelf.

cious.——

cious.—He had left the houfe before it occurred to me in the ftrong light it does now, or I fhould have told him fo—My poverty makes me proud—I will not be infulted by a fuperficial puppy.—His intimacy with Mifs ——— gave him a privilege, which he fhould not have affumed with me—a propofal might be made to his coufin, a milliner's girl, which fhould not have been mentioned to me. Pray tell him that I am offended —and do not wifh to fee him again !— When I meet him at your houfe, I fhall leave the room, fince I cannot pull him by the nofe. I can force my fpirit to leave my body—but it fhall never bend to fupport that body—God of heaven, fave thy child from this living death !— I fcarcely know what I write. My hand trembles—I am very fick—fick at heart.———

MARY.

LETTER XII.

Tuesday Evening.

Sir,

WHEN you left me this morning, and I reflected a moment—your *officious* message, which at first appeared to me a joke—looked so very like an insult—I cannot forget it—To prevent then the necessity of forcing a smile—when I chance to meet you—I take the earliest opportunity of informing you of my real sentiments.

MARY WOLLSTONECRAFT.

LETTER

LETTER XIII.

Wednesday, 3 o'clock.

Sir,

IT is inexpreffibly difagreeable to me to be obliged to enter again on a fubject, that has already raifed a tumult of *indignant* emotions in my bofom, which I was labouring to fupprefs when I received your letter. I fhall now *condefcend* to anfwer your epiftle ; but let me firft tell you, that, in my *unprotected* fituation, I make a point of never forgiving a *deliberate infult*—and in that light I confider your late officious conduct. It is not according to my nature to mince matters—I will then tell you in

plain

plain terms, what I think. I have ever confidered you in the light of a *civil* acquaintance—on the word friend I lay a peculiar emphafis—and, as a mere acquaintance, you were rude and *cruel*, to ftep forward to infult a woman, whofe conduct and misfortunes demand refpect. If my friend, Mr. Johnfon, had made the propofal—I fhould have been feverely hurt—have thought him unkind and unfeeling, but not *impertinent*.—The privilege of intimacy you had no claim to—and fhould have referred the man to myfelf—if you had not fufficient difcernment to quafh it at once. I am, fir, poor and deftitute.—Yet I have a fpirit that will never bend, or take indirect methods, to obtain the confequence I defpife ; nay, if to fupport life it was neceffary to act contrary to my principles, the ftruggle would

would foon be over. I can bear any thing but my own contempt.

In a few words, what I call an infult, is the bare fuppofition that I could for a moment think of *proftituting* my perfon for a maintenance; for in that point of view does fuch a marriage appear to me, who confider right and wrong in the abftract, and never by words and local opinions fhield myfelf from the reproaches of my own heart and underftanding.

It is needlefs to fay more—Only you muft excufe me when I add, that I wifh never to fee, but as a perfect ftranger, a perfon who could fo grofsly miftake my character. An apology is not neceffary—if you were inclined to make one—nor any further expoftulations.— I again repeat, I cannot overlook an affront; few indeed have fufficient delicacy

licacy to refpect poverty, even where
it gives luftre to a character—and I tell
you fir, I am POOR—yet can live without your benevolent exertions.

MARY WOLLSTONECRAFT.

———————

LETTER XIV.

I SEND you *all* the books I had to re-
view except Dr. J—'s Sermons, which
I have begun. If you wifh me to look
over any more trafh this month—you
muft fend it directly. I have been fo
low-fpirited fince I faw you—I was
quite glad, laft night, to feel myfelf affected by fome paffages in Dr. J—'s
fermon on the death of his wife—I
seemed

feemed (fuddenly) to *find* my *foul* again
—It has been for fome time I cannot
tell where. Send me the Speaker—
and *Mary*, I want one—and I fhall foon
want fome paper—you may as well
fend it at the fame time—for I am try-
ing to brace my nerves that I may be
induftrious.—I am afraid reafon is not a
good bracer—for I have been reafoning
a long time with my untoward fpirits—
and yet my hand trembles.—I could
finifh a period very *prettily* now, by faying that it ought to be fteady when I
add that I am yours fincerely,

MARY.

If you do not like the manner in
which I reviewed Dr. J—'s f—— on
his wife, be it known unto you—I *will*
not do it any other way—I felt fome
pleafure in paying a juft tribute of refpect

fpect to the memory of a man—who,
fpite of his faults, I have an affection
for—I fay *have*, for I believe he is
fomewhere—*where* my foul has been
gadding perhaps;—but *you* do not live
on conjectures.

LETTER XV.

My dear fir, I fend you a chapter
which I am pleafed with, now I fee it
in one point of view—and, as I have
made free with the author, I hope you
will not have often to fay—what does
this mean?

You forgot you were to make out
my

my account—I am, of courſe, over
head and ears in debt ; but I have not
that kind of pride, which makes ſome
diſlike to be obliged to thoſe they re-
ſpeɛt.—On the contrary, when I involuntarily lament that I have not a father
or brother, I thankfully recolleɛt that
I have received unexpeɛted kindneſs
from you and a few others.—So reaſon
allows, what nature impels me to—for
I cannot live without loving my fellow-
creatures—nor can I love them, without diſcovering ſome virtue.

MARY.

LETTER

nances, fhouldering their arms. About
nine o'clock this morning, the king
paffed by my window, moving filently
along (excepting now and then a few
ftrokes on the drum, which rendered
the ftillnefs more awful) through empty
ftreets, furrounded by the national guards,
who, cluftering round the carriage,
feemed to deferve their name. The
inhabitants flocked to their windows,
but the cafements were all fhut, not a
voice was heard, nor did I fee any
thing like an infulting gefture.—For
the firft time fince I entered France,
I bowed to the majefty of the people,
and refpected the propriety of behaviour
fo perfectly in unifon with my own
feelings. I can fcarcely tell you why,
but an affociation of ideas made the
tears flow infenfibly from my eyes,
when I faw Louis fitting, with more
dignity

dignity than I expected from his character, in a hackney coach, going to
meet death, where so many of his race
have triumphed. My fancy instantly
brought Louis XIV before me, entering the capital with all his pomp, after
one of the victories most flattering to
his pride, only to fee the sunshine of
prosperity overshadowed by the sublime
gloom of misery. I have been alone
ever since; and, though my mind is
calm, I cannot dismiss the lively images
that have filled my imagination all the
day.—Nay, do not smile, but pity me;
for, once or twice, lifting my eyes from
the paper, I have seen eyes glare
through a glass-door opposite my chair
and bloody hands shook at me. Not
the distant sound of a footstep can I
hear.—My apartments are remote from
those of the servants, the only persons
who

who sleep with me in an immense hotel,
one folding door opening after another.
—I wish I had even kept the cat with
me!—I want to see something alive;
death in so many frightful shapes has
taken hold of my fancy.—I am going to
bed—and, for the first time in my life, I
cannot put out the candle.

M. W.

EXTRACT

OF THE

CAVE OF FANCY.

A TALE.

[*Begun to be written in the year* 1787, *but never completed*]

CAVE OF FANCY.

CHAP. I.

YE who expect conftancy where every
thing is changing, and peace in the
midft of tumult, attend to the voice of
experience, and mark in time the foot-
fteps of difappointment, or life will be
loft in defultory wifhes, and death arrive before the dawn of wifdom.

In a fequeftered valley, furrounded by
rocky mountains that intercepted many
of the paffing clouds, though funbeams
variegated their ample fides, lived a
fage, to whom nature had unlocked

her

her moſt hidden ſecrets. His hollow
eyes, ſunk in their orbits, retired from
the view of vulgar objects, and turned
inwards, overleaped the boundary pre-
ſcribed to human knowledge. Intenſe
thinking during fourſcore and ten years,
had whitened the ſcattered locks on
his head, which, like the ſummit of
the diſtant mountain, appeared to be
bound by an eternal froſt.

On the ſandy waſte behind the mountains, the track of ferocious beaſts
might be traced, and ſometimes the
mangled limbs which they left, attracted
a hovering flight of birds of prey. An
extenſive wood the ſage had forced to
rear its head in a ſoil by no means congenial, and the firm trunks of the trees
ſeemed to frown with defiance on time;
though the ſpoils of innumerable ſum-
mers covered the roots, which reſembled
fangs;

fangs; fo clofely did they cling to the
unfriendly fand, where ferpents hiffed,
and fnakes, rolling out their vaft folds,
inhaled the noxious vapours. The ra-
vens and owls who inhabited the folitude, gave alfo a thicker gloom to the
everlafting twilight, and the croaking
of the former a monotony, in unifon
with the gloom; whilft lions and tygers,
fhunning even this faint femblance of
day, fought the dark caverns, and at
night, when they fhook off fleep, their
roaring would make the whole valley
refound, confounded with the fcreech-
ings of the bird of night.

One mountain rofe fublime, towering
above all, on the craggy fides of which
a few fea-weeds grew, wafhed by the
ocean, that with tumultuous roar rufhed to affault, and even undermine, the
huge barrier that ftopped its progrefs;
and

and ever and anon a ponderous mafs, loofened from the cliff, to which it fcarcely feemed to adhere, always threatening to fall, fell into the flood, rebounding as it fell, and the found was re-echoed from rock to rock. Look where you would, all was without form, as if nature, fuddenly ftopping her hand, had left chaos a retreat.

Clofe to the moft remote fide of it was the fage's abode. It was a rude hut, formed of ftumps of trees and matted twigs, to fecure him from the inclemency of the weather; only through fmall apertures croffed with ruſhes, the wind entered in wild murmurs, modulated by thefe obftructions. A clear fpring broke out of the middle of the adjacent rock, which, dropping flowly into a cavity it had hollowed, foon overflowed, and then ran, ftruggling to

free

free itfelf from the cumbrous fragments, till, become a deep, filent ftream, it efcaped through reeds, and roots of trees, whofe blafted tops overhung and darkened the current.

One fide of the hut was fupported by the rock, and at midnight, when the fage ftruck the inclofed part, it yawned wide, and admitted him into a cavern in the very bowels of the earth, where never human foot before had trod; and the various fpirits, which inhabit the different regions of nature, were here obedient to his potent word. The cavern had been formed by the great inundation of waters, when the approach of a comet forced them from their fource; then, when the fountains of the great deep were broken up, a ftream rufhed out of the centre of the earth, where the fpirits, who have lived

on

on it, are confined to purify themfelves from the drofs contracted in their firft ftage of exiftence; and it flowed in black waves, for ever bubbling along the cave, the extent of which had never been explored. From the fides and top, water diftilled, and, petrifying as it fell, took fantaftic fhapes, that foon divided it into apartments, if fo they might be called. In the foam, a wearied fpirit would fometimes rife, to catch the moft diftant glimpfe of light, or tafte the vagrant breeze, which the yawning of the rock admitted, when Sageftus, for that was the name of the hoary fage, entered. Some, who were refined and almoft cleared from vicious fpots, he would allow to leave, for a limited time, their dark prifon-houfe; and, flying on the winds acrofs the bleak northern ocean, or rifing in an exhalation

tion till they reached a fun-beam, they thus re-vifited the haunts of men. Thefe were the guardian angels, who in foft whifpers reftrain the vicious, and animate the wavering wretch who ftands fufpended between virtue and vice.

Sageftus had fpent a night in the cavern, as he often did, and he left the filent veftibule of the grave, juft as the fun, emerging from the ocean, difperfed the clouds, which were not half fo denfe as thofe he had left. All that was human in him rejoiced at the fight of reviving life, and he viewed with pleafure the mounting fap rifing to expand the herbs, which grew fpontaneoufly in this wild—when, turning his eyes towards the fea, he found that death had been at work during his abfence, and terrific marks of a furious ftorm ftill fpread horror around. Though the

the day was ferene, and threw bright
rays on eyes for ever fhut, it dawned
not for the wretches who hung pendent
on the craggy rocks, or were ftretched
lifelefs on the fand. Some, ftruggling,
had dug themfelves a grave; others
had refigned their breath before the
impetuous furge whirled them on fhore.
A few, in whom the vital fpark was
not fo foon diflodged, had clung to
loofe fragments; it was the grafp of
death; embracing the ftone, they ftiff-
ened; and the head, no longer erect,
refted on the mafs which the arms en-
circled. It felt not the agonizing gripe,
nor heard the figh that broke the heart
in twain.

Refting his chin on an oaken club,
the fage looked on every fide, to fee
if he could difcern any who yet breathed. He drew nearer, and thought he
faw,

faw, at the firft glance, the unclofed eyes glare; but foon perceived that they were a mere glaffy fubftance, mute as the tongue; the jaws were fallen, and, in fome of the tangled locks, hands were clinched; nay, even the nails had entered fharpened by defpair. The blood flew rapidly to his heart; it was flefh; he felt he was ftill a man, and the big tear paced down his iron cheeks, whofe mufcles had not for a long time been relaxed by fuch humane emotions. A moment he breathed quick, then heaved a figh, and his wonted calm returned with an unaccuftomed glow of tendernefs; for the ways of heaven were not hid from him; he lifted up his eyes to the common Father of nature, and all was as ftill in his bofom, as the fmooth deep, after having clofed

over

over the huge veſſel from which the wretches had fled.

Turning round a part of the rock that jutted out, meditating on the ways of Providence, a weak infantine voice reached his ears; it was liſping out the name of mother. He looked, and beheld a blooming child leaning over, and kiſſing with eager fondneſs, lips that were infenſible to the warm preſſure. Starting at the fight of the ſage, ſhe fixed her eyes on him, " Wake her, ah! wake her," ſhe cried, " or the ſea will catch us." Again he felt compaſſion, for he ſaw that the mother ſlept the ſleeþ of death. He ſtretched out his hand, and, ſmoothing his brow, invited her to approach; but ſhe ſtill intreated him to wake her mother, whom ſhe continued to call, with an impatient tremulous voice. To detach

her

her from the body by perſuaſion would not have been very eaſy. Sageſtus had a quicker method to effect his purpoſe ; he took out a box which contained a ſoporific powder, and as ſoon as the fumes reached her brain, the powers of life were ſuſpended.

He carried her directly to his hut, and left her ſleeping profoundly on his ruſhy couch.

CHAP.

C H A P. II.

AGAIN Sageſtus approached the
dead, to view them with a more ſcruti-
nizing eye. He was perfectly ac-
quainted with the conſtruction of the
human body, knew the traces that virtue or vice leaves on the whole frame;
they were now indelibly fixed by death;
nay more, he knew by the ſhape of
the ſolid ſtructure, how far the ſpirit
could range, and ſaw the barrier beyond
which it could not paſs: the mazes of
fancy he explored, meaſured the ſtretch
of thought, and, weighing all in an
even balance, could tell whom nature
had ſtamped an hero, a poet, or phi-
loſopher.

By

By their appearance, at a tranfient glance, he knew that the veffel muft have contained many paffengers, and that fome of them were above the vulgar, with refpect to fortune and education ; he then walked leifurely among the dead, and narrowly obferved their pallid features.

His eye firft refted on a form in which proportion reigned, and, ftroking back the hair, a fpacious forehead met his view; warm fancy had revelled there, and her airy dance had left veftiges, fcarcely vifible to a mortal eye. Some perpendicular lines pointed out that melancholy had predominated in his conftitution ; yet the ftraggling hairs of his eye-brows fhowed that anger had often fhook his frame; indeed, the four temperatures, like the four elements, had refided in this little world,
and

and produced harmony. The whole
vifage was bony, and an energetic
frown had knit the flexible fkin of his
brow; the kingdom within had been
extenfive; and the wild creations of
fancy had there "a local habitation
and a name." So exquifite was his
fenfibility, fo quick his comprehenfion,
that he perceived various combinations
in an inftant; he caught truth as fhe
darted towards him, faw all her fair
proportion at a glance, and the flafh of
his eye fpoke the quick fenfes which
conveyed intelligence to his mind; the
fenforium indeed was capacious, and
the fage imagined he faw the lucid
beam, fparkling with love or ambition,
in charaɛters of fire, which a graceful
curve of the upper eyelid fhaded. The
lips were a little deranged by contempt; and a mixture of vanity and
                                    felf-

LETTER XVI.

Paris, December 26, 1792.

I SHOULD immediately on the receipt of your letter, my dear friend, have thanked you for your punctuality, for it highly gratified me, had I not wished to wait till I could tell you that this day was not ftained with blood. Indeed the prudent precautions taken by the National Convention to prevent a tumult, made me fuppofe that the dogs of faction would not dare to bark, much lefs to bite, however true to their fcent; and I was not miftaken; for the citizens, who were all called out, are returning home with compofed counte-
nances,

felf-complacency formed a few irregular lines round them. The chin had fuffered from fenfuality, yet there were ftill great marks of vigour in it, as if advanced with ftern dignity. The hand accuftomed to command, and even tyrannize, was unnerved; but its appearance convinced Sageftus, that he had oftener wielded a thought than a weapon; and that he had filenced, by irrefiftible conviction, the fuperficial difputant, and the being, who doubted becaufe he had not ftrength to believe, who, wavering between different borrowed opinions, firft caught at one ftraw, then at another, unable to fettle into any confiftency of character. After gazing a few moments, Sageftus turned away exclaiming, How are the ftately oaks torn up by a tempeft, and the bow

unftrung

unftrung, that could force the arrow
beyond the ken of the eye!

What a different face next met his
view! The forehead was fhort, yet well
fet together; the nofe fmall, but a little
turned up at the end; and a draw-down
at the fides of his mouth, proved that
he had been a humourift, who minded
the main chance, and could joke with
his acquaintance, while he eagerly de-
voured a dainty which he was not to
pay for. His lips fhut like a box whofe
hinges had often been mended; and
the mufcles, which difplay the foft emotion of the heart on the cheeks, were
grown quite rigid, fo that, the veffels
that fhould have moiftened them not
having much communication with the
grand fource of paffions, the fine volatile fluid had evaporated, and they
became mere dry fibres, which might

be

be pulled by any misfortune that threatened himfelf, but were not fufficiently elaftic to be moved by the miferies of others. His joints were inferted compactly, and with celerity they had performed all the animal functions, without any of the grace which refults from the imagination mixing with the fenfes.

A huge form was ftretched near him, that exhibited marks of overgrown infancy; every part was relaxed; all appeared imperfect. Yet, fome undulating lines on the puffed-out cheeks, difplayed figns of timid, fervile good nature; and the fkin of the forehead had been fo often drawn up by wonder, that the few hairs of the eyebrows were fixed in a fharp arch, whilft an ample chin refted in lobes of flefh on his protuberant breaft.

By

By his fide was a body that had
fcarcely ever much life in it—fympathy
feemed to have drawn them together—
every feature and limb was round and
fiefhy, and, if a kind of brutal cunning
had not marked the face, it might have
been miftaken for an automaton, fo unmixed was the phlegmatic fluid. The
vital fpark was buried deep in a foft
mafs of matter, refembling the pith in
young elder, which, when found, is fo
equivocal, that it only appears a moift-
er part of the fame body.

Another part of the beach was
covered with failors, whofe bodies exhibited marks of ftrength and brutal
courage.—Their characters were all
different, though of the fame clafs;
Sageftus did not ftay to difcriminate
them, fatisfied with a rough fketch.
He faw indolence roufed by a love of
humour,

humour, or rather bodily fun; fenfuality and prodigality with a vein of generofity running through it; a contempt
of danger with grofs fuperftition;
fupine fenfes, only to be kept alive by
noify, tumultuous pleafures, or that
kind of novelty which borders on ab-
furdity: this formed the common out-
line, and the reft were rather dabs than
fhades.

Sageftus paufed, and remembered it
had been faid by an earthly wit, that
" many a flower is born to blufh un-
feen, and wafte its fweetnefs on the
defart air." How little, he exclaimed,
did that poet know of the ways of
heaven! And yet, in this refpect, they
are direct; the hands before me, were
defigned to pull a rope, knock down a
fheep, or perform the fervile offices of
life; no " mute, inglorious poet" refts
amongft

amongſt them, and he who is ſuperior
to his fellow, does not riſe above mediocrity.   The genius that ſprouts from
a dunghil ſoon ſhakes off the hetero-
genous maſs; thoſe only grovel, who
have not power to fly.

He turned his ſtep towards the mother of the orphan : another female
was at ſome diſtance ; and a man who,
by his garb, might have been the hufband, or brother, of the former, was
not far off.

Him the ſage ſurveyed with an attentive eye, and bowed with reſpect
to the inanimate clay, that lately had
been the dwelling of a moſt benevolent
ſpirit.   The head was ſquare, though
the features were not very prominent;
but there was a great harmony in every
part, and the turn of the noſtrils and
lips evinced, that the ſoul muſt have
had

had tafte, to which they had ferved as
organs. Penetration and judgment
were feated on the brows that overhung the eye. Fixed as it was, Sageftus quickly difcerned the expreffion
it muft have had; dark and penfive,
rather from flownefs of comprehenfion
than melancholy, it feemed to abforb
the light of knowledge, to drink it in
ray by ray; nay, a new one was not
allowed to enter his head till the laft
was arranged : an opinion was thus
cautioufly received, and maturely
weighed, before it was added to the
general ftock. As nature led him to
mount from a part to the whole, he
was moft converfant with the beautiful,
and rarely comprehended the fublime;
yet, faid Sageftus, with a foftened tone,
he was all heart, full of forbearance, and
defirous to pleafe every fellow-creature;
but

but from a nobler motive than a love
of admiration; the fumes of vanity
never mounted to cloud his brain, or
tarnish his beneficence. The fluid in
which those placid eyes swam, is now
congealed; how often has tendernefs
given them the fineft water! Some
torn parts of the child's drefs hung
round his arm, which led the fage to
conclude, that he had faved the child;
every line in his face confirmed the
conjecture; benevolence indeed ftrung
the nerves that naturally were not
very firm; it was the great knot that
tied together the fcattered qualities,
and gave the diftinct ftamp to the character.

The female whom he next approached, and fuppofed to be an attendant on
the other, was below the middle fize,
and her legs were fo difproportionably
                                    fhort,

ſhort, that, when ſhe moved, ſhe muſt
have waddled along; her elbows were
drawn in to touch her long taper, waiſt,
and the air of her whole body was an
affectation of gentility. Death could
not alter the rigid hang of her limbs, or
efface the ſimper that had ſtretched her
mouth; the lips were thin, as if nature
intended ſhe ſhould mince her words;
her noſe was ſmall, and ſharp at the
end; and the forehead, unmarked by
eyebrows, was wrinkled by the diſcon-
tent that had ſunk her cheeks, on
which Sageſtus ſtill diſcerned faint
traces of tenderneſs; and fierce good-
nature, he perceived had ſometimes
animated the little ſpark of an eye that
anger had oftener lighted. The ſame
thought occurred to him that the ſight
of the ſailors had ſuggeſted, Men and
women are all in their proper places—
this

this female was intended to fold up linen and nurfe the fick.

Anxious to obferve the mother of his charge, he turned to the lily that had been fo rudely fnapped, and, carefully obferving it, traced every fine line to its fource. There was a delicacy in her form, fo truly feminine, that an involuntary defire to cherifh fuch a being, made the fage again feel the almoft forgotten fenfations of his nature. On obferving her more clofely, he difcovered that her natural delicacy had been increafed by an improper education, to a degree that took away all vigour from her faculties. And its baneful influence had had fuch an effect on her mind, that few traces of the exertions of it appeared on her face, though the fine finifh of her features, and particularly the form of the forehead, convinced

vinced the fage that her underftanding might have rifen confiderably above mediocrity, had the wheels ever been put in motion; but, clogged by preju- dices, they never turned quite round, and, whenever fhe confidered a fubject, fhe ftopped before fhe came to a con- clufion. Affuming a mafk of pro- priety, fhe had banifhed nature; yet its tendency was only to be diverted, not ftifled. Some lines, which took from the fymmetry of the mouth, not very obvious to a fuperficial obferver, ftruck Sageftus, and they appeared to him characters of indolent obftinacy. Not having courage to form an opinion of her own, fhe adhered, with blind partiality, to thofe fhe adopted, which fhe received in the lump, and, as they always remained unopened, of courfe fhe only faw the even glofs on the out- fide.

fide. Veftiges of anger were vifible on her brow, and the fage concluded, that fhe had often been offended with, and indeed would fcarcely make any allowance for, thofe who did not coincide with her in opinion, as things always appear felf-evident that have never been examined ; yet her very weaknefs gave a charming timidity to her countenance ; goodnefs and tendernefs pervaded every lineament, and melted in her dark blue eyes. The compaffion that wanted activity, was fincere, though it only embellifhed her face, or produced cafual acts of charity when a moderate alms could relieve prefent diftrefs. Unacquainted with life, fictitious, unnatural diftrefs drew the tears that were not fhed for real mifery. In its own fhape, human wretchednefs excites a little difguft in the mind that

has

has indulged fickly refinement. Perhaps the fage gave way to a little conjecture in drawing the laft conclufion ;
but his conjectures generally arofe from
diftinct ideas, and a dawn of light
allowed him to fee a great way farther
than common mortals.

He was now convinced that the orphan was not very unfortunate in having
loft fuch a mother. The parent that
infpires fond affection without refpect,
is feldom an ufeful one ; and they only
are refpectable, who confider right and
wrong abftracted from local forms and
accidental modifications.

Determined to adopt the child, he
named it after himfelf, Sagefta, and
retired to the hut where the innocent
flept, to think of the beft method of
educating this child, whom the angry
deep had fpared.

[The

[The laſt branch of the education of
Sageſta, conſiſted of a variety of cha-
raƈters and ſtories preſented to her
in the Cave of Fancy, of which the
following is a ſpecimen.]

CHAP.

CHAP.

A FORM now approached that particularly ftruck and interefted Sagefta. The fage, obferving what paffed in her mind, bade her ever truft to the firft impreffion. In life, he continued, try to remember the effect the firft appearance of a ftranger has on your mind; and, in proportion to your fenfibility, you may decide on the character. Intelligence glances from eyes that have the fame purfuits, and a benevolent heart foon traces the marks of benevolence on the countenance of an unknown fellow-creature; and not only the countenance, but the geftures, the

voice,

voice, loudly fpeak truth to the unpre-
judiced mind.

Whenever a ftranger advances towards you with a tripping ftep, receives
you with broad fmiles, and a profufion
of compliments, and yet you find yourfelf embarraffed and unable to return
the falutation with equal cordiality, be
affured that fuch a perfon is affected,
and endeavours to maintain a very good
character in the eyes of the world,
without really practifing the focial virtues which drefs the face in looks of
unfeigned complacency. Kindred minds
are drawn to each other by expreffions
which elude defcription ; and, like the
calm ·breeze that plays on a fmooth
lake, they are rather felt than feen.
Beware of a man who always appears in
good humour; a felfifh defign too frequently lurks in the fmiles the heart

never

never curved; or there is an affectation
of candour that deftroys all ftrength of
character, by blending truth and falf-
hood into an unmeaning mafs. The
mouth, in fact, feems to be the feature
where you may trace every kind of dif-
fimulation, from the fimper of vanity,
to the fixed fmile of the defigning villain. Perhaps, the modulations of
the voice will ftill more quickly give
a key to the character than even the
turns of the mouth, or the words
that iffue from it; often do the
tones of unpractifed diffemblers give
the lie to their affertions. Many
people never fpeak in an unnatural
voice, but when they are infincere: the
phrafes not correfponding with the
dictates of the heart, have nothing to
keep them in tune. In the courfe of
an argument however, you may eafily
difcover whether vanity or conviction
                              ftimulates

ftimulates the difputant, though his
inflated countenance may be turned
from you, and you may not fee the
geftures which mark felf-fufficiency.
He ftopped, and the fpirit began.

I have wandered through the cave;
and, as foon as I have taught you a ufeful leffon, I fhall take my flight where
my tears will ceafe to flow, and where
mine eyes will no more be fhocked
with the fight of guilt and forrow.
Before many moons have changed,
thou wilt enter, O mortal! into that
world I have lately left. Liften to my
warning voice, and truft not too much
to the goodnefs which I perceive refides
in thy breaft. Let it be reined in by
principles, left thy very virtue fharpen
the fting of remorfe, which as naturally
follows diforder in the moral world, as
pain attends on intemperance in the
phyfical.

phyfical. But my hiftory will afford you
more inftruction than mere advice. Sageftus concurred in opinion with her,
obferving that the fenfes of children
fhould be the firft object of improvement;
then their paffions worked on; and judgment the fruit, muft be the acquire-
ment of the being itfelf, when out of
leading-ftrings. The fpirit bowed af-
fent, and, without any further prelude,
entered on her hiftory.

My mother was a moft refpectable
character, but fhe was yoked to a man
whofe follies and vices made her ever
feel the weight of her chains. The
firft fenfation I recollect, was pity; for
I have feen her weep over me and the
reft of her babes, lamenting that the
extravagance of a father would throw
us deftitute on the world. But, though
my father was extravagant, and feldom
thought

thought of any thing but his own pleafures, our education was not neglected.
In folitude, this employment was my
mother's only folace; and my father's
pride made him procure us mafters;
nay, fometimes he was fo gratified by
our improvement, that he would em-
brace us with tendernefs, and intreat
my mother to forgive him, with marks
of real contrition. But the affection his
penitence gave rife to, only ferved to
expofe her to continual difappointments, and keep hope alive merely to
torment her. After a violent debauch
he would let his beard grow, and the
fadnefs that reigned in the houfe I fhall
never forget; he was afhamed to meet
even the eyes of his children. This is fo
contrary to the nature of things, it
gave me exquifite pain; I ufed, at thofe
times, to fhow him extreme refpect. I
could

could not bear to fee my parent humble himfelf before me. However neither his conftitution, nor fortune could long bear the conftant wafte. He had, I have obferved, a childifh affection for his children, which was difplayed in careffes that gratified him for the moment, yet never reftrained the head-long fury of his appetites ; his momentary repentance wrung his heart, without influencing his conduct ; and he died, leaving an encumbered wreck of a good eftate.

As we had always lived in fplendid poverty, rather than in affluence, the fhock was not fo great ; and my mother repreffed her anguifh, and concealed fome circumftances, that fhe might not fhed a deftructive mildew over the gaiety of youth.

So fondly did I doat on this dear pa-rent,

rent, that she engroſſed all my tenderneſs; her ſorrows had knit me firmly to
her, and my chief care was to give her
proofs of affection. The gallantry that
afforded my companions, the few young
people my mother forced me to mix
with, ſo much pleaſure, I deſpiſed; I
wiſhed more to be loved than admired,
for I could love. I adored virtue; and
my imagination, chaſing a chimerical
object, overlooked the common pleaſures
of life; they were not ſufficient for my
happineſs. A latent fire made me burn
to riſe ſuperior to my contemporaries in
wiſdom and virtue; and tears of joy
and emulation filled my eyes when I
read an account of a great action—I
felt admiration, not aſtoniſhment.

My mother had two particular friends,
who endeavoured to ſettle her affairs;
one was a middle-aged man, a merchant;

chant; the human breaſt never en-
ſhrined a more benevolent heart. His
manners were rather rough, and he
bluntly ſpoke his thoughts without ob-
ſerving the pain it gave; yet he poſſeſſ-
ed extreme tenderneſs, as far as his diſ-
cernment went. Men do not make
ſufficient diſtinction, ſaid ſhe, digreſſing
from her ſtory to addreſs Sageſtus, between tenderneſs and ſenſibility.

To give the ſhorteſt definition of ſenſibility, replied the ſage, I ſhould ſay
that it is the reſult of acute ſenſes, finely
faſhioned nerves, which vibrate at the
ſlighteſt touch, and convey ſuch clear intelligence to the brain, that it does not
require to be arranged by the judgment.
Such perſons inſtantly enter into the
characters of others, and inſtinctively
diſcern what will give pain to every
human being; their own feelings are

fo

fo varied that they feem to contain in themfelves, not only all the paffions of the fpecies, but their various modifications. Exquifite pain and pleafure is their portion; nature wears for them a different afpect than is difplayed to common mortals. One moment it is a paradife; all is beautiful: a cloud arifes, an emotion receives a fudden damp; darknefs invades the fky, and the world is an unweeded garden;—but go on with your narrative, faid Sageftus, recollecting himfelf.

She proceeded. The man I am defcribing was humanity itfelf; but frequently he did not underftand me; many of my feelings were not to be analyzed by his common fenfe. His friendfhips, for he had many friends, gave him pleafure unmixed with pain; his religion was coldly reafonable, becaufe he want-

ed

ed fancy, and he did not feel the neceffity of finding, or creating, a perfect
object, to anfwer the one engraved on
his heart: the fketch there was faint.
He went with the ftream, and rather
caught a character from the fociety he
lived in, than fpread one around him.
In my mind many opinions were graven
with a pen of brafs, which he thought
chimerical: but time could not erafe
them, and I now recognize them as
the feeds of eternal happinefs: they
will foon expand in thofe realms where
I fhall enjoy the blifs adapted to my
nature; this is all we need afk of the
Supreme Being; happinefs muft follow
the completion of his defigns. He
however could live quietly, without
giving a preponderancy to many important opinions that continually ob-
truded on my mind; not having an enthufiaftic

thufiaftic affection for his fellow creatures, he did them good, without fuffering from their follies. He was particularly attached to me, and I felt for
him all the affection of a daughter;
often, when he had been interefting
himfelf to promote my welfare, have I
lamented that he was not my father;
lamented that the vices of mine had
dried up one fource of pure affection.

The other friend I have already alluded to, was of a very different character; greatnefs of mind, and thofe
combinations of feeling which are fo
difficult to defcribe, raifed him above
the throng, that buftle their hour out,
lie down to fleep, and are forgotten.
But I fhall foon fee him, fhe exclaimed,
as much fuperior to his former felf, as
he then rofe in my eyes above his fellow creatures! As fhe fpoke, a glow
of

of delight animated each feature; her countenance appeared tranfparent; and fhe filently anticipated the happinefs fhe fhould enjoy, when fhe entered thofe manfions, where death-divided friends fhould meet, to part no more; where human weaknefs could not damp their blifs, or poifon the cup of joy that, on earth, drops from the lips as foon as tafted, or, if fome daring mortal fnatches a hafty draught, what was fweet to the tafte becomes a root of bitternefs.

He was unfortunate, had many cares to ftruggle with, and I marked on his cheeks traces of the fame forrows that funk my own. He was unhappy I fay, and perhaps pity might firft have awoke my tendernefs; for, early in life, an artful woman worked on his compaf-fionate foul, and he united his fate to a being made up of fuch jarring ele-ments,

ments, that he was ftill alone. The difcovery did not extinguifh that propenfity to love, a high fenfe of virtue fed. I faw him fick and unhappy, without a friend to footh the hours languor made heavy; often did I fit a long winter's evening by his fide, railing at the fwift wings of time, and terming my love, humanity.

Two years paffed in this manner, filently rooting my affection; and it might have continued calm, if a fever had not brought him to the very verge of the grave. Though ftill deceived, I was miferable that the cuftoms of the world did not allow me to watch by him; when fleep forfook his pillow, my wearied eyes were not clofed, and my anxious fpirit hovered round his bed. I faw him, before he had recovered his ftrength; and, when his hand touched mine,

mine, life almoſt retired, or flew to meet the touch. The firſt look found a ready way to my heart, and thrilled through every vein. We were left alone, and infenfibly began to talk of the immortality of the foul; I declared that I could not live without this con-viction. In the ardour of converſation he preſſed my hand to his heart; it reſted there a moment, and my emo-tions gave weight to my opinion, for the affection we felt was not of a pe-riſhable nature.—A filence enfued, I know not how long; he then threw my hand from him, as if it had been a ferpent; formally complained of the weather, and adverted to twenty other uninterefting fubjects. Vain efforts! Our hearts had already fpoken to each other.

Feebly did I afterwards combat an affection,

affection, which feemed twifted in every fibre of my heart. The world ftood ftill when I thought of him; it moved heavily at beft, with one whofe very conftitution feemed to mark her out for mifery. But I will not dwell on the paffion I too fondly nurfed. One only refuge had I on earth; I could not refolutely defolate the fcene my fancy flew to, when worldly cares, when a knowledge of mankind, which my circumftances forced on me, rendered every other infipid. I was afraid of the unmarked vacuity of common life; yet, though I fupinely indulged myfelf in fairy-land, when I ought to have been more actively employed, virtue was ftill the firft mover of my actions; fhe dreffed my love in fuch enchanting colours, and fpread the net I could never break. Our correfponding feelings confounded

our

our very fouls; and in many converfations we almoft intuitively difcerned
each other's fentiments; the heart opened itfelf, not chilled by referve, nor
afraid of mifconftruction. But, if virtue
infpired love, love gave new energy to
virtue, and abforbed every felfifh paffion. Never did even a wifh efcape
me, that my lover fhould not fulfil the
hard duties which fate had impofed on
him. I only diffembled with him in
one particular; I endeavoured to foften
his wife's too confpicuous follies, and
extenuated her failings in an indirect
manner. To this I was prompted by a
loftinefs of fpirit; I fhould have broken
the band of life, had I ceafed to refpect
myfelf. But I will haften to an important change in my circumftances.

My mother, who had concealed the
real ftate of her affairs from me, was
now

now impelled to make me her confident, that I might affift to difcharge
her mighty debt of gratitude. The
merchant, my more than father, had
privately affifted her: but a fatal civil-
war reduced his large property to a
bare competency; and an inflammation
in his eyes, that arofe from a cold he
had caught at a wreck, which he watch-
ed during a ftormy night to keep off
the lawlefs colliers, almoft deprived
him of fight. His life had been fpent
in fociety, and he fcarcely knew how
to fill the void; for his fpirit would not
allow him to mix with his former
equals as an humble companion; he
who had been treated with uncommon
refpeft, could not brook their infulting
pity. From the refource of folitude,
reading, the complaint in his eyes cut
im

him off, and he became our conftant vifitor.

Actuated by the fincereft affection, I ufed to read to him, and he miftook my tendernefs for love. How could I undeceive him, when every circumftance frowned on him! Too foon I found that I was his only comfort; I, who rejected his hand when fo tune fmiled, could not now fecond her blow; and, in a moment of enthufiaftic gratitude and tender compaffion, I offered him my hand.—It was received with pleafure; tranfport was not made for his foul; nor did he difcover that nature had feparated us, by making me alive to fuch different fenfations. My mother was to live with us, and I dwelt on this circumftance to banifh cruel recollections, when the bent bow returned to its former ftate.

With

With a burſting heart and a firm
voice, I named the day when I was to
ſeal my promiſe. It came, in ſpite of
my regret; I had been previouſly preparing myſelf for the awful ceremony,
and anſwered the ſolemn queſtion with
a reſolute tone, that would ſilence the
dictates of my heart; it was a forced,
unvaried one; had nature modulated
it, my ſecret would have eſcaped. My
active ſpirit was painfully on the watch
to repreſs every tender emotion. The
joy in my venerable parent's countenance, the tenderneſs of my huſband,
as he conducted me home, for I really
had a ſincere affection for him, the gra-
tulations of my mind, when I thought
that this ſacrifice was heroic, all tended
to deceive me; but the joy of victory
over the reſigned, pallid look of my
lover, haunted my imagination, and
fixed

fixed itfelf in the centre of my brain.—
Still I imagined, that his fpirit was near
me, that he only felt forrow for my
lofs, and without complaint refigned
me to my duty.

I was left alone a moment; my two
elbows refted on a table to fupport my
chin. Ten thoufand thoughts darted
with aftonifhing velocity through my
mind. My eyes were dry; I was on the
brink of madnefs. At this moment a
ftrange affociation was made by my
imagination; I thought of Gallileo, who
when he left the inquifition, looked
upwards, and cried out, "Yet it moves."
A fhower of tears, like the refrefhing
drops of heaven, relieved my parched
fockets; they fell difregarded on the
table; and, ftamping with my foot, in an
agony I exclaimed, " Yet I love." My
hufband entered before I had calmed
thefe

thefe tumultuous emotions, and tenderly took my hand. I fnatched it from
him; grief and furprife were marked
on his countenance; I haftily ftretched
it out again. My heart fmote me, and I
removed the tranfient mift by an unfeigned endeavour to pleafe him.

A few months after, my mind grew
calmer; and, if a treacherous imagination, if feelings many accidents revived, fometimes plunged me into melancholy, I often repeated with fteady
conviction, that virtue was not an
empty name, and that, in following the
dictates of duty, I had not bidden adieu
to content.

In the courfe of a few years, the
dear object of my fondeft affection,
faid farewel, in dying accents. Thus
left alone, my grief became dear; and I
did not feel folitary, becaufe I thought
I might,

I might, without a crime, indulge a paffion, that grew more ardent than ever when my imagination only prefented him to my view, and reftored my former activity of foul which the late calm had rendered torpid. I feemed to find myfelf again, to find the eccentric warmth that gave me identity of character. Reafon had governed my conduct, but could not change my nature; this voluptuous forrow was fuperior to every gratification of fenfe, and death more firmly united our hearts.

Alive to every human affection, I fmoothed my mother's paffage to eternity, and fo often gave my hufband fincere proofs of affection, he never fuppofed that I was actuated by a more fervent attachment. My melancholy, my uneven fpirits, he attributed to my extreme fenfibility, and loved me the

better

better for poffeffing qualities he could
not comprehend.

At the clofe of a fummer's day, fome
years after, I wandered with carelefs
fteps over a pathlefs common; various
anxieties had rendered the hours which
the fun had enlightened heavy; fober
evening came on; I wifhed to ftill " my
mind, and woo lone quiet in her filent
walk." The fcene accorded with my
feelings; it was wild and grand; and
the fpreading twilight had almoft confounded the diftant fea with the barren,
blue hills that melted from my fight.
I fat down on a rifing ground; the rays
of the departing fun illumined the ho-
rizon, but fo indiftinctly, that I anticipated their total extinction. The
death of Nature led me to a ftill more
interefting fubject, that came home to
my bofom, the death of him I loved.
A village-

A village-bell was tolling; I liftened, and thought of the moment when I heard his interrupted breath, and felt the agonizing fear, that the fame found would never more reach my ears, and that the intelligence glanced from my eyes, would no more be felt. The fpoiler had feized his prey; the fun was fled, what was this world to me! I wandered to another, where death and darknefs could not enter; I purfued the fun beyond the mountains, and the foul efcaped from this vale of tears. My reflections were tinged with melancholy, but they were fublime.— I grafped a mighty whole, and fmiled on the king of terrors; the tie which bound me to my friends he could not break; the fame myfterious knot united me to the fource of all goodnefs and happinefs. I had feen the divinity reflected

flected in a face I loved; I had read
immortal characters difplayed on a
human countenance, and forgot myfelf
whilft I gazed. I could not think of
immortality, without recollecting the
ecftacy I felt, when my heart firft whif-
pered to me that I was beloved; and
again did I feel the facred tie of mutual
affection; fervently I prayed to the father of mercies; and rejoiced that he
could fee every turn of a heart, whofe
movements I could not perfectly underftand. My paffion feemed a pledge
of immortality; I did not wifh to hide
it from the all-fearching eye of heaven.
Where indeed could I go from his prefence? and, whilft it was dear to me,
though darknefs might reign during
the night of life, joy would come when
I awoke to life everlafting.

I now turned my ftep towards home,
when

when the appearance of a girl, who
ftood weeping on the common, attracted my attention. I accofted her,
and foon heard her fimple tale; that her
father was gone to fea, and her mother
fick in bed. I followed her to their
little dwelling, and relieved the fick
wretch. I then again fought my own
abode; but death did not now haunt
my fancy. Contriving to give the poor
creature I had left more effectual relief,
I reached my own garden-gate very
weary, and refted on it.—Recollecting
the turns of my mind during the walk,
I exclaimed, Surely life may thus be
enlivened by active benevolence, and
the fleep of death, like that I am now
difpofed to fall into, may be fweet!

My life was now unmarked by any
extraordinary change, and a few days
ago

ago I entered this cavern; for through
it every mortal muſt paſs; and here I
have diſcovered, that I neglected many
opportunities of being uſeful, whilſt I
foſtered a devouring flame. Remorſe
has not reached me, becauſe I firmly
adhered to my principles, and I have
alſo diſcovered that I ſaw through a
falſe medium. Worthy as the mortal
was I adored, I ſhould not long have
loved him with the ardour I did, had
fate united us, and broken the deluſion
the imagination ſo artfully wove. His
virtues, as they now do, would have
extorted my eſteem; but he who formed
the human ſoul, only can fill it, and the
chief happineſs of an immortal being
muſt ariſe from the ſame ſource as its
exiſtence. Earthly love leads to heavenly, and prepares us for a more exalted

alted ſtate; if it does not change its
nature, and deſtroy itſelf, by trampling
on the virtue, that conſtitutes its eſſence,
and allies us to the Deity.

ON

POETRY,

AND

OUR RELISH FOR THE BEAUTIES OF NATURE.

ON

POETRY, &c.

———————

A TASTE for rural fcenes, in the prefent ftate of fociety, appears to be very often an artificial fentiment, rather infpired by poetry and romances, than a real perception of the beauties of nature. But, as it is reckoned a proof of refined tafte to praife the calm pleafures which the country affords, the theme is never exhaufted. Yet it may be made a queftion, whether this ro-

mantic

mantic kind of declamation, has much effect on the conduct of thofe, who leave, for a feafon, the crowded cities in which they were bred.

I have been led to thefe reflections, by obferving, when I have refided for any length of time in the country, how few people feem to contemplate nature with their own eyes. I have " brufhed the dew away" in the morning; but, pacing over the printlefs grafs, I have wondered that, in fuch delightful fitu-ations, the fun was allowed to rife in folitary majefty, whilft my eyes alone hailed its beautifying beams. The webs of the evening have ftill been fpread acrofs the hedged path, unlefs fome labouring man, trudging to work, difturbed the fairy ftructure; yet, in fpite of th's fupinenefs, when I joined

the

the focial circle, every tongue rang changes on the pleafures of the country.

Having frequently had occafion to make the fame obfervation, I was led to endeavour, in one of my folitary rambles, to trace the caufe, and likewife to enquire why the poetry written in the infancy of fociety, is moft natural: which, ftrictly fpeaking (for *natural* is a very indefinite expreffion) is merely to fay, that it is the tranfcript of immediate fenfations, in all their native wildnefs and fimplicity, when fancy, awakened by the fight of interefting objects, was moft actively at work. At fuch moments, fenfibility quickly furnifhes fimiles, and the fublimated fpirits combine images, which rifing fpontaneoufly, it is not neceffary coldly to ranfack the underftanding or memory, till the laborious efforts of judgment

ment exclude prefent fenfations, and damp the fire of enthufiafm.

The effufions of a vigorous mind, will ever tell us how far the underftanding has been enlarged by thought, and ftored with knowledge. The richnefs of the foil even appears on the furface; and the refult of profound thinking, often mixing, with playful grace, in the reveries of the poet, fmoothly incorpo-rates with the ebullitions of animal fpirits, when the finely fafhioned nerve vibrates acutely with rapture, or when, relaxed by foft melancholy, a pleafing languor prompts the long-drawn figh, and feeds the flowly falling tear.

The poet, the man of ftrong feelings, gives us only an image of his mind, when he was actually alone, converfing with himfelf, and marking the im-preffion which nature had made on his

own

own heart.—If, at this facred moment, the idea of fome departed friend, fome tender recollection when the foul was moft alive to tendernefs, intruded un-awares into his thoughts, the forrow which it produced is artlefsly, yet po-etically expreffed—and who can avoid fympathizing?

Love to man leads to devotion—grand and fublime images ftrike the imagination—God is feen in every floating cloud, and comes from the mifty mountain to receive the nobleft homage of an intelligent creature—praife. How folemn is the moment, when all affections and remembrances fade before the fublime admiration which the wifdom and goodnefs of God infpires, when he is worfhipped in a *temple not made with hands*, and the world feems to contain only the mind that

that formed, and the mind that con-
templates it!   Thefe are not the weak
refponfes of ceremonial devotion; nor,
to exprefs them, would the poet need
another poet's aid : his heart burns
within him, and he fpeaks the language of truth and nature with refift-
lefs energy.

Inequalities, of courfe, are obferv-
able in his effufions; and a lefs vigorous fancy, with more tafte, would
have produced more elegance and uni-
formity; but, as paffages are foftened
or expunged during the cooler moments of reflection, the underftanding
is gratified at the expence of thofe involuntary fenfations, which, like the
beauteous tints of an evening fky, are
fo evanefcent, that they melt into new
forms before they can be analyzed. For
however eloquently we may boaft of
                                                    our

our reafon, man muft often be delighted he cannot tell why, or his blunt
feelings are not made to relifh the beauties which nature, poetry, or any of
the imitative arts, afford.

The imagery of the ancients feems
naturally to have been borrowed from
furrounding objects and their mytho-
logy. When a hero is to be tranfport-
ed from one place to another, acrofs
pathlefs waftes, is any vehicle fo natural, as one of the fleecy clouds on which
the poet has often gazed, fcarcely con-
fcious that he wifhed to make it his
chariot? Again, when nature feems
to prefent obftacles to his progrefs at
almoft every ftep, when the tangled
foreft and fteep mountain ftand as bar-
riers, to pafs over which the mind
longs for fupernatural aid; an inter-
pofing deity, who walks on the waves,
and

and rules the ftorm, feverely felt in the
firft attempts to cultivate a country,
will receive from the impaffioned fancy
" a local habitation and a name."

It would be a philofophical enquiry,
and throw fome light on the hiftory of
the human mind, to trace, as far as our
information will allow us to trace, the
fpontaneous feelings and ideas which
have produced the images that now
frequently appear unnatural, becaufe
they are remote; and difgufting, becaufe they have been fervilely copied
by poets, whofe habits of thinking,
and views of nature muft have been
different; for, though the underftanding
feldom difturbs the current of our prefent feelings, without diffipating the
gay clouds which fancy has been embracing, yet it filently gives the colour
to the whole tenour of them, and the

dream

dream is over, when truth is grofsly
violated, or images introduced, felected
from books, and not from local manners
or popular prejudices.

In a more advanced ftate of civilization, a poet is rather the creature of
art, than of nature. The books that he
reads in his youth, become a hot-bed
in which artificial fruits are produced,
beautiful to the common eye, though
they want the true hue and flavour.
His images do not arife from fenfations;
they are copies; and, like the works
of the painters who copy ancient fta-
tues when they draw men and women
of their own times, we acknowledge
that the features are fine, and the pro-
portions juft; yet they are men of
ftone; infipid figures, that never convey to the mind the idea of a portrait
taken from life, where the foul gives

fpirit

fpirit and homogeneity to the whole.
The filken wings of fancy are fhrivel-
led by rules; and a defire of attaining
elegance of diction, occafions an attention to words, incompatible with
fublime, impaffioned thoughts.

A boy of abilities, who has been
taught the ftructure of verfe at fchool,
and been roufed by emulation to compofe rhymes whilft he was reading
works of genius, may, by practice,
produce pretty verfes, and even become what is often termed an elegant
poet: yet his readers, without knowing what to find fault with, do not
find themfelves warmly interefted. In
the works of the poets who faften on
their affections, they fee groffer faults,
and the very images which fhock their
tafte in the modern; ftill they do not appear as puerile or extrinfic in one as the
other.—

other.—Why?—becaufe they did not appear fo to the author.

It may found paradoxical, after obferving that thofe productions want vigour, that are merely the work of imitation, in which the underftanding has violently directed, if not extinguifhed, the blaze of fancy, to affert, that, though genius be only another word for exquifite fenfibility, the firft obfervers of nature, the true poets, exercifed their underftanding much more than their imitators. But they exercifed it to difcriminate things, whilft their followers were bufy to borrow fentiments and arrange words.

Boys who have received a claffical education, load their memory with words, and the correfpondent ideas are perhaps never diftinctly comprehended. As a proof of this affertion,

I muft

I muſt obſerve, that I have known many young people who could write tolerably ſmooth verſes, and ſtring epithets prettily together, when their proſe themes ſhowed the barrenneſs of their minds, and how ſuperficial the cultivation muſt have been, which their underſtanding had received.

Dr. Johnſon, I know, has given a definition of genius, which would overturn my reaſoning, if I were to admit it.—He imagines, that *a ſtrong mind, accidentally led to ſome particular ſtudy in* which it excels, is a genius.—Not to ſtop to inveſtigate the cauſes which produced this happy *ſtrength* of mind, experience ſeems to prove, that thoſe minds have appeared moſt vigorous, that have purſued a ſtudy, after nature had diſcovered a bent; for it would be abſurd to ſuppoſe, that a ſlight impreſ-

ſion

fion made on the weak faculties of a
boy, is the fiat of fate, and not to be
effaced by any fucceeding impreffion,
or unexpected difficulty. Dr. Johnfon
in fact, appears fometimes to be of the
fame opinion (how confiftently I fhall
not now enquire), efpecially when he
obferves, " that Thomfon looked on
nature with the eye which fhe only
gives to a poet."

But, though it fhould be allowed
that books may produce fome poets, I
fear they will never be the poets who
charm our cares to fleep, or extort admiration. They may diffufe tafte, and
polifh the language ; but I am inclined
to conclude that they will feldom roufe
the paffions, or amend the heart.

And, to return to the firft fubject of
difcuffion, the reafon why moft people
are more interefted by a fcene defcribed

ed by a poet, than by a view of nature,
probably arifes from the want of a
lively imagination. The poet contracts
the profpect, and, felecting the moft
picturefque part in his *camera*, the judgment is directed, and the whole force
of the languid faculty turned towards
the objects which excited the moft
forcible emotions in the poet's heart;
the reader confequently feels the enlivened defcription, though he was not
able to receive a firft impreffion from
the operations of his own mind.

Befides, it may be further obferved,
that grofs minds are only to be moved
by forcible reprefentations. To roufe
the thoughtlefs, objects muft be prefented, calculated to produce tumultuous emotions; the unfubftantial, picturefque forms which a contemplative
man gazes on, and often follows with
                              ardour

ardour till he is mocked by a glimpfe of unattainable excellence, appear to them the light vapours of a dreaming enthufiaft, who gives up the fubftance for the fhadow. It is not within that they feek amufement; their eyes are feldom turned on themfelves; confequently their emotions, though fometimes fervid, are always tranfient, and the nicer perceptions which diftinguifh the man of genuine tafte, are not felt, or make fuch a flight impreffion as fcarcely to excite any pleafurable fenfations. Is it furprifing then that they are often overlooked, even by thofe who are delighted by the fame images concentrated by the poet?

But even this numerous clafs is exceeded, by witlings, who, anxious to appear to have wit and tafte, do not allow their underftandings or feel-

ings

ings any liberty; for, inftead of cultivating their faculties and reflecting on
their operations, they are bufy collect-
ing prejudices; and are predetermined
to admire what the fuffrage of time
announces as excellent, not to ftore up
a fund of amufement for themfelves,
but to enable them to talk.

Thefe hints will affift the reader to
trace fome of the caufes why the beauties of nature are not forcibly felt,
when civilization, or rather luxury,
has made confiderable advances—thofe
calm fenfations are not fufficiently
lively to ferve as a relaxation to the vo-
luptuary, or even to the moderate pur-
fuer of artificial pleafures. In the prefent ftate of fociety, the underftanding
muft bring back the feelings to nature,
or the fenfibility muft have fuch native
ftrength, as rather to be whetted than
deftroyed

deftroyed by the ftrong exercifes of paffion.

That the moft valuable things are liable to the greateft perverfion, is however as trite as true :—for the fame fenfibility, or quicknefs of fenfes, which makes a man relifh the tranquil fcenes of nature, when fenfation, rather than reafon, imparts delight, frequently makes a libertine of him, by leading him to prefer the fenfual tumult of love a little refined by fentiment, to the calm pleafures of affectionate friendfhip, in whofe fober fatisfactions, reafon, mixing her tranquillizing convictions, whifpers, that content, not happinefs, is the reward of virtue in this world.

H I N T S.

[Chiefly designed to have been incorporated in the Second Part of the Vindication of the Rights of Woman.]

H I N T S.

1.

INDOLENCE is the fource of ner‑
vous complaints, and a whole hoft of
cares. This devil might fay that his
name was legion.

2.

It fhould be one of the employments
of women of fortune, to vifit hofpitals,
and fuperintend the conduct of inferiors.

3.

It is generally fuppofed, that the
imagination of women is particularly
active,

active, and leads them astray. Why then do we seek by education only to exercise their imagination and feeling, till the understanding, grown rigid by disuse, is unable to exercise itself— and the superfluous nourishment the imagination and feeling have received, renders the former romantic, and the latter weak?

4.

Few men have risen to any great eminence in learning, who have not received something like a regular education. Why are women expected to surmount difficulties that men are not equal to?

5.

Nothing can be more absurd than the ridicule of the critic, that the heroine of his mock-tragedy was in love with the very man whom she ought
leaft

leaſt to have loved; he could not have given a better reaſon. How can paſſion gain ſtrength any other way? In Ota‐heite, love cannot be known, where the obſtacles to irritate an indiſcrimi‐nate appetite, and ſublimate the ſimple ſenſations of deſire till they mount to paſſion, are never known. There a man or woman cannot love the very perſon they ought not to have loved—nor does jealouſy ever fan the flame.

6.

It has frequently been obſerved, that, when women have an object in view, they purſue it with more ſteadineſs than men, particularly love. This is not a compliment. Paſſion purſues with more heat than reaſon, and with moſt ardour during the abſence of reaſon.

7.

Men are more ſubject to the phyſical love

love than women.   The confined education of women makes them more
fubject to jealoufy.

8.

Simplicity feems, in general, the confequence of ignorance, as I have obferved in the characters of women and
failors—the being confined to one track
of impreffions.

9.

I know of no other way of preferving the chaftity of mankind, than that
of rendering women rather objects of
love than defire.   The difference is
great.   Yet, while women are encou-
raged to ornament their perfons at the
expence of their minds, while indolence renders them helplefs and lafci-
vious (for what other name can be
given to the common intercourfe between the fexes?) they will be, generally

rally fpeaking, only objeds of defire;
and, to fuch women, men cannot be
conflant. Men, accuftomed only to
have their fenfes moved, merely feek
for a felfifh gratification in the fociety
of women, and their fexual inftinct,
being neither fupported by the underftanding nor the heart, muft be excited
by variety.

10.

We ought to refpect old opinions;
though prejudices, blindly adopted,
lead to error, and preclude all exercife
of the reafon.

The emulation which often makes a
boy mifchievous, is a generous fpur;
and the old remark, that unlucky, tur-
bulent boys, make the wifeft and beft
men, is true, fpite of Mr. Knox's arguments. It has been obferved, that the
moft adventurous horfes, when tamed

or.

or domefticated, are the moft mild and tractable.

11.

The children who ftart up fuddenly at twelve or fourteen, and fall into decays, in confequence, as it is termed, of outgrowing their ftrength, are in general, I believe, thofe children, who have been bred up with miftaken tendernefs, and not allowed to fport and take exercife in the open air. This is analogous to plants: for it is found that they run up fickly, long ftalks, when confined.

12.

Children fhould be taught to feel deference, not to practife fubmiffion.

13.

It is always a proof of falfe refinement, when a faftidious tafte overpowers fympathy.

14. Luft

14.

Luft appears to be the moft natural companion of wild ambition ; and love of human praife, of that dominion erected by cunning.

15.

" Genius decays as judgment in- creafes." Of courfe, thofe who have the leaft genius, have the earlieft ap- pearance of wifdom.

16.

A knowledge of the fine arts, is fel- dom fubfervient to the promotion of either religion or virtue. Elegance is often indecency ; witnefs our prints.

17.

There does not appear to be any evil in the world, but what is neceffary. The doctrine of rewards and punifh- ments, not confidered as a means of re- formation,

formation, appears to me an infamous. libel on divine goodnefs.

18.

Whether virtue is founded on reafon or revelation, virtue is wifdom, and vice is folly. Why are pofitive punifh-ments?

19.

Few can walk alone. The ftaff of Chriftianity is the neceffary fupport of human weaknefs. But an acquaint-ance with the nature of man and virtue, with juft fentiments on the attributes, would be fufficient, without a voice from heaven, to lead fome to virtue, but not the mob.

20.

I only expect the natural reward of virtue, whatever it may be. I rely not on a pofitive reward.

The juftice of God can be vindicated
by

by a belief in a future ſtate—but a con-
tinuation of being vindicates it as
clearly, as the poſitive ſyſtem of rewards and puniſhments—by evil educ-
ing good for the individual, and not
for an imaginary whole. The happineſs of the whole muſt ariſe from the
happineſs of the conſtituent parts, or
this world is not a ſtate of trial, but a
ſchool.

21.

The vices acquired by Auguſtus to
retain his power, muſt have tainted his
ſoul, and prevented that increaſe of
happineſs a good man expects in the
next ſtage of exiſtence. This was a
natural puniſhment.

22.

The lover is ever moſt deeply en-
amoured, when it is with he knows
not what—and the devotion of a myſtic
has

has a rude Gothic grandeur in it, which the refpectful adoration of a philofopher will never reach. I may be thought fanciful; but it has continually occurred to me, that, though, I allow, reafon in this world is the mother of wifdom—yet fome flights of the imagination feem to reach what wifdom cannot teach—and, while they delude us here, afford a glorious hope, if not a foretafte, of what we may expect hereafter. He that created us, did not mean to mark us with ideal images of grandeur, the *bafelefs fabric of a vifion*— No—that perfection we follow with hopelefs ardour when the whifperings of reafon are heard, may be found, when not incompatible with our ftate, in the round of eternity. Perfection indeed muft, even then, be a comparative idea—but the wifdom, the happinefs

pinefs of a fuperior ftate, has been fuppofed to be intuitive, and the happieft
effufions of human genius have feemed
like infpiration—the deductions of reafon deftroy fublimity.

23.

I am more and more convinced, that
poetry is the firft effervefcence of the
imagination, and the forerunner of civilization.

24.

When the Arabs had no trace of li-
terature or fcience, they compofed
beautiful verfes on the fubjects of love
and war. The flights of the imagination, and the laboured deductions of
reafon, appear almoft incompatible.

25.

Poetry certainly flourifhes moft in
the firft rude ftate of fociety. The
paffions fpeak moft eloquently, when
they are not fhackled by reafon. The
fublime

fublime expreffion, which has been fo
often quoted, [Genefis, ch. 1, ver. 3.]
is perhaps a barbarous flight ; or rather
the grand conception of an uncultivat-
ed mind ; for it is contrary to nature
and experience, to fuppofe that this
account is founded on facts—It is
doubtlefs a fublime allegory. But a
cultivated mind would not thus have
defcribed the creation—for, arguing
from analogy, it appears that creation
muft have been a comprehenfive plan,
and that the Supreme Being always
ufes fecond caufes, flowly and filently
to fulfil his purpofe. This is, in reality,
a more fublime view of that power
which wifdom fupports : but it is not
the fublimity that would ftrike the impaffioned mind, in which the imagination took place of intellect. Tell a
being, whofe affections and paffions
have been more exercifed than his rea-
son,

fon, that God faid, *Let there be light!
and there was light*; and he would prof-
trate himfelf before the Being who
could thus call things out of nothing,
as if they were: but a man in whom
reafon had taken place of paffion,
would not adore, till wifdom was confpicuous as well as power, for his admiration muft be founded on principle.

26.

Individuality is ever confpicuous in
thofe enthufiaftic flights of fancy, in
which reafon is left behind, without
being loft fight of.

27.

The mind has been too often brought
to the teft of enquiries which only
reach to matter—put into the crucible,
though the magnetic and electric fluid
efcapes from the experimental philofopher.

28. Mr.

28.

Mr. Kant has obferved, that the underftanding is fublime, the imagination
beautiful—yet it is evident, that poets,
and men who undoubtedly poffefs the
livelieft imagination, are moft touched
by the fublime, while men who have
cold, enquiring minds, have not this
exquifite feeling in any great degree,
and indeed feem to lofe it as they cultivate their reafon.

29.

The Grecian buildings are graceful—
they fill the mind with all thofe pleafing
emotions, which elegance and beauty
never fail to excite in a cultivated
mind—utility and grace ftrike us in
unifon—the mind is fatisfied—things
appear juft what they ought to be: a
calm fatisfaction is felt, but the imagination has nothing to do—no obfcurity
darkens

darkens the gloom—like reafonable content, we can fay why we are pleaf- ed—and this kind of pleafure may be lafting, but it is never great.

30.

When we fay that a perfon is an original, it is only to fay in other words that he thinks. " The lefs a man has " cultivated his rational faculties, the " more powerful is the principle of " imitation, over his actions, and his " habits of thinking. Moft women, " of courfe, are more influenced by " the behaviour, the fafhions, and the " opinions of thofe with whom they " affociate, than men." (Smellie.)

When we read a book which fup- ports our favourite opinions, how ea- gerly do we fuck in the doctrines, and fuffer our minds placidly to reflect the images which illuftrate the tenets we

have

have embraced? We indolently or quietly acquiefce in the conclufion, and our fpirit animates and connects the various fubjects. But, on the contrary, when we perufe a fkilful writer, who does not coincide in opinion with us, how is the mind on the watch to detect fallacy? And this coolnefs often prevents our being carried away by a ftream of eloquence, which the prejudiced mind terms declamation—a pomp of words.—We never allow ourfelves to be warmed; and, after contending with the writer, are more confirmed in our own opinion, as much perhaps from a fpirit of contradiction as from reafon.—Such is the ftrength of man!

31.

It is the individual manner of feeing and feeling, pourtrayed by a ftrong imagination in bold images that have

ftruck

ftruck the fenfes, which creates all the charms of poetry. A great reader is always quoting the defcription of another's emotions; a ftrong imagination delights to paint its own. A writer of genius makes us feel; an inferior author reafon.

32.

Some principle prior to felf-love muft have exifted : the feeling which produced the pleafure, muft have exifted before the experience.

THE END.